A SCRAPBOOK *of*

MOTHERHOOD FIRSTS

Stories to Celebrate & Wisdom to Bless Moms

THE WORD QUILTERS
Leslie Wilson
Trish Berg
Terra Hangen
Cathy Messecar
Karen Robbins

LEAFWOOD
PUBLISHERS

A Scrapbook of Motherhood Firsts

Stories to Celebrate and Wisdom to Bless Moms

Copyright 2012 by The Word Quilters

ISBN 978-0-915547-71-5

Printed in the United States of America

Scripture quotations, unless otherwise noted, are from The Holy Bible, New International Version. Copyright 1984, International Bible Society.

Used by permission of Zondervan Publishers.

Library of Congress Cataloging-in-Publication Data
A scrapbook of motherhood firsts : stories to celebrate and wisdom
to bless moms / The Word Quilters, Leslie Wilson ... [et al.].
       p. cm.
ISBN 978-0-915547-71-5
1. Motherhood—Religious aspects—Christianity—
Miscellanea. I. Wilson, Leslie (Leslie Porter)
BV4529.18.S398 2012
242'.6431—dc23
2011052275

Cover and Interior Design: Thinkpen Design, Inc., www.thinkpendesign.com

Leafwood Publishers is an imprint of
Abilene Christian University Press
1626 Campus Court
Abilene, Texas 79601
1-877-816-4455

www.leafwoodpublishers.com

12 13 14 15 16 17 / 7 6 5 4 3 2 1

Contents

4

Foreword

Motherhood.

Combine the slogan of the Peace Corps—The Toughest Job You'll Ever Love—with the *Survivor* mantra—Outwit, Outplay, Outlast—and you begin to have a feel for the magnitude and challenge of the profession. If women truly weighed the physical, emotional, and mental demands of motherhood, they might opt out before they start. But moms choose not to dwell on the downsides. Instead, we celebrate the blessing of rearing offspring *because* of the challenges.

From the moment we hold that wrinkly infant belting out screams heard half a mile away, from the moment we sign those adoption papers declaring us legally to be what we've already purposed in our hearts, we fall deeply in love.

We rejoice in taking on every aspect of mothering—whether it be diapering, nursing, feeding, bathing, changing, rocking, disciplining, tucking in, teaching, nurturing, reading, singing, cooking, laundering, carpooling, counseling—realizing that we're the perfect match for our particular children.

Along the way, we moms tend to mark our baby's firsts. We carefully record milestones in our child's baby book—things like the first tooth, first steps, first words, first haircut, first playdate, first day of school, first soccer game, first car, first love. We take hundreds (millions?) of pictures to record these firsts, including getting ears pierced, starring in the school play, going to the ER, getting a driver's license, and graduating high school.

This book, co-authored by five columnists who call themselves the Word Quilters, recalls those life-impacting moments that women celebrate to congratulate moms on a job well done.

Family Snapshot essays highlight heartwarming events that moved from mundane to spectacular precisely because they were a child's first. In some, we poke fun at our naïveté. Others will make you shed tears of joy or recognition.

A Few of Our Favorite Things spotlights the Word Quilters' special memories of preferred gifts, family traditions, and outdoor activities.

Yummy, Yummy in My Tummy shares favorite family recipes—foods that real kids will actually eat.

In *Word Quilters' Wisdom,* the authors share their most valuable advice—things someone passed on to them that enriched motherhood or made it easier, or things they wished they had known but learned the hard way!

Mommy's Little Helps includes tried-and-true tips for every generation. Who couldn't use some help in the areas of discipline, travel, organization, or saving money and time?

Mama Sez recalls timeless quotes from authors, speakers, leaders, and performers known around the world.

Nourishment for Mom's Spirit ties in appropriate verses from Scripture.

Mom Miscellany captures all the stuff that didn't fit into the other categories. Great fun!

You Might Be a Mommy If . . . makes real moms feel normal. Truthfully, once we acknowledge that we won't sleep through the night until our child is three years old and that we will do nearly fifteen thousand loads of laundry before our youngest goes off to college, we begin to relax and feel more comfortable with the task we've been given.

We're excited you're joining us as we celebrate you—your work as a mom, your passion, your joys, and the ups and downs. By recalling those award-winning memories every mom tucks away in her heart, we share the excitement we have for our chosen career. So please know this, you're the Bestest Mommy in the Whole Wide World. Way to go, Mom!

CHAPTER ONE

Getting the Party Started

Mama Sez

Mother is the name for God on the lips and hearts of little children.

—WILLIAM MAKEPEACE THACKERAY

FAMILY SNAPSHOT

A Whisper in the Wind

BY TRISH BERG

Motherhood did not sneak up on me like a whisper in the wind. Mike and I had been married for over two years when we decided it was time to start a family. Sadly, our timing didn't line up with God's timing. Big surprise, huh? We'd been trying to get pregnant for over six months when I decided we needed help. My OB/GYN suggested we begin basal temperature monitoring, time our romantic encounters, and systematically take control of the situation.

About six months later, the little stick turned blue. We then went through seven months of a glorious, much-wanted pregnancy only to discover that life sometimes does sneak up on you when you least expect it.

One day while standing in the grocery store checkout line, it hit me. Once our baby arrived, our lives would never be the same again. I didn't faint, though I suddenly felt light-headed. I may have looked calm on the outside, but on the inside I had a panic attack.

That night, Mike turned to me and said, "Trish, I'm not sure I'm ready to be a dad."

Not ready? What was he saying? Okay, now I experienced a full-fledged nervous breakdown! If I didn't know how to be a mom, and he didn't know how to be a dad, how in the world could the two of us raise this baby?

I guess we spent so much time preparing for the pregnancy that we forgot about the baby's birth. In that single moment, I realized that pregnancy didn't signal an end, but a beginning—an entrance, not an exit. No one had ever told me that, and I guess it took me a bit by surprise.

Years later, I discovered most moms feel apprehensive. Every first-time mom has no idea what she's doing. Yet God created us to be mothers. So when that panicked feeling hits, know that God planned for you to be a mom.

Rest assured that God would not make a mistake. So take a deep breath, Mom. The party is just getting started.

. . Word Quilters' Wisdom . .

DO AS I SAY, NOT AS I DID

CATHY
Buy only flushable pets.

KAREN
Don't worry over small things. Save it for the larger issues.

LESLIE
Consistently provide a variety of foods for your children, so they'll learn
to enjoy many different flavors, textures, colors, and ethnic varieties.

TERRA
I taught our sons to be kind to all living critters, and together we captured spiders
in our house and set them free outside, saved bees from drowning in the birdbath,
and gently moved worms out of the way when gardening. But oh, I have a dark side
and declared war on snails in our garden, offering a bounty of one penny per snail. So
the humble snail was left out of my "be kind to all critters" teaching.

TRISH
Keep after-school snacks in a special drawer
in the fridge, easy to grab and healthy to eat.

Inconceivable

BY LESLIE WILSON

*A*fter our son Charlie's birth, my husband, Bret, and I struggled to get pregnant again. I found myself an enigma—women who had no children couldn't understand my sorrow over my secondary infertility.

Like many infertile women, I noticed humungous bellies everywhere I went. It seemed every other woman on the planet was with child—that child being still in utero, dragged alongside mama, or pushed in a stroller. I avoided baby showers and any event or venue where I might run into pregnant women. Every Mother's Day was bittersweet—yes, I felt fortunate to have Charlie, but God had placed in me the desire to have more children. In my darkest of dark infertility moments, I vomited upon learning that one of my closest friends was pregnant.

I found solace in a support group, finally able to vent my emotions about the ups and downs of being unable to conceive. Bret and I learned that we had to become our own advocates. No one would care about or do as much about our infertility as we would.

For those of you who haven't been through it, infertility can squeeze love and intimacy out of the reproduction picture. In fact, on the morning after my husband made his "deposit" for our artificial insemination, he had to leave for work immediately.

"Can't you stay until Dr. Heckman finishes the procedure?" I said. I wanted Bret to be in the room when his sperm fertilized my egg. I'm just funny that way.

"I wish I could, but I really need to get to this meeting," he said, smooching my lips, then my forehead.

I pouted before, during, and after the procedure. His swimmers—oblivious to my sour attitude—motored toward their Nirvana.

After the intrauterine insemination was over, Dr. Heckman joked, "It was good for me. Was it good for you?"

I was even less amused when he offered me a cigarette.

Two excruciatingly long weeks passed.

The OB/GYN who had done my IUI checked my HCG levels and called me ASAP. My numbers weren't off the charts, but for the first time in years of trying, we had a glimmer of hope.

With God, nothing is inconceivable.

Mama Sez

When you are a mother, you are never really alone in your thoughts.
A mother always has to think twice, once for herself and once for her child.

—SOPHIA LOREN

. . *Word Quilters' Wisdom* . .

WHAT I LEARNED THROUGH ADVERSITY

KAREN

While it may not be a lot of comfort at the time through some of those difficult phases of growing up, I learned that "this too will pass."

LESLIE

Prepare the child for the path—not the path for the child.

TERRA

I learned to lean on Jesus when my son was hit by a car and taken to the ER, with a possible broken leg and back injury. I'd never prayed that hard or long! Thankfully, we took our son home that day, his leg in a cast, and my heart thanking Jesus for our son's recovery.

CATHY

One morning, my exhausted sister Sherry, who was caring for two toddlers, placed them in a near-vacant playroom in her home. She lay down with pillow and blanket in the doorway to create a human barrier and corral the kids in that safe zone. Often fatigued, I learned that a good night of rest or a power nap benefitted me more than an empty kitchen sink or perfectly made beds. I vote for *Webster's Dictionary* to use the word "motherhood" to define "exhausting." Now go take a nap.

TRISH

I enjoy biking on the country roads near our home. When I approach a hill, it always looks so steep and impossible until I get closer and see that the slope isn't so bad after all. One pedal at a time, I make it up to the top. The hills we must climb in life are the same, fearfully steep until we walk by faith up the slope. And God helps us pedal.

Morning Sickness

By Leslie Wilson

My easy pregnancy with Baby Number One lulled me into a false sense of security. Not once did I feel sick. Sleepless nights and indigestion left me alone. I didn't have hemorrhoids and didn't develop stretch marks. The birth itself—complete with epidural—seemed easy compared to the horror stories I'd heard.

This idyllic first experience left me ill-prepared for my pregnancy with Baby Number Two. That time through, I got to experience everything cliché about pregnancy, from hormones to heartburn. Plus, I developed morning sickness.

I have no idea why experts call it that. My queasiness lasted all day—until week fifteen of my pregnancy. And I wasn't just nauseous, either. I actually vomited four or five times a day. My OB/GYN worried about my baby's health with my lack of weight gain.

Each sickness episode played out the same. I'd struggle to keep down my cookies—praying for deliverance in some form or fashion. I counted to one hundred, simply holding my hands over my mouth, to no avail. Waiting until the last possible second, I'd propel from the couch, bounding toward the hall bath—which was also my son's bathroom. Lifting the toilet seat, I heaved—barely making it.

Then I'd chide myself for employing such a foolish *modus operandi*: "You know you're gonna be sick. Why do you lie on the couch for so long, taking the risk of barfing all over the floor or sofa? Just go to the bathroom and get it over with."

The next time, I'd wait, ever hopeful the ill feelings might pass. They didn't.

This went on hour after hour, day after day, week after week. Bret tolerated my routine, slamming up against walls if necessary to move out of my way. I felt sorrier for Charlie, my three-year-old son, who had to endure my rocket launches without reprieve.

Bless his little heart, Charlie took to imitating me. Every now and then, he would purposefully lie down on the couch, moan and groan for a few seconds, and then sprint to his bathroom. Once inside, he completed the routine by making retching sounds, flushing the toilet, closing the lid, then sitting on it to cry. When family members wanted a chuckle, they'd prompt Charlie to "show us what Mommy does."

All the illness and challenges of the first half of the pregnancy faded when little Molly arrived. She was the best baby—rarely cried, loved to snuggle, slept, and ate well from the start. So much so that I feared I was being lulled into another false sense of security . . .

MOM MISCELLANY
IF YOU GIVE A MOM A MINUTE

By Trish Berg

*J*f you give a mom a minute, she'll probably want a cup of tea. When you get her the tea, she'll probably want a lemon crumb muffin to go with it. When you give her the lemon crumb muffin, she'll want to sit in the big comfy chair and relax. Sitting in the big comfy chair will remind her to put her feet up. Once she puts her feet up, she'll notice that her feet are cold. She'll run and get her warm, fuzzy slippers.

Then she'll decide to read a good book. As she opens the book, she starts to feel guilty that she hasn't read her devotional for the day. So she'll get out her Bible. As she reads her devotional, she'll be reminded that her biggest blessings are in the playroom playing all alone, and the silence could be a warning sign.

So she'll get up off the big comfy chair, put down her muffin, and walk over to the playroom to check on her children. That's when her stomach will begin to grumble as she realizes that it's almost suppertime, and she has no idea what to make. So she'll head into the kitchen to make something for supper. Going into the kitchen will remind her that she never did the breakfast or lunch dishes. So she'll take a deep breath and begin to load the dishwasher.

Loading the dishwasher will remind her that she left a plate in the family room with her lemon crumb muffin on it. So she'll head out to the family room to get it. As she approaches the big comfy chair, she notices that there are crumbs all over the carpet, since her biggest blessings ate the muffin and weren't very neat about it.

The crumbs on the carpet will remind her that she needs to run the sweeper. As she walks to the closet to get the sweeper, she passes by the kitchen and notices she accidentally left the water running. At full sprint, she'll hit the faucet just before the water spills over the edge of the sink. As she turns the water off, she'll notice the lemon crumb muffins in the Tupperware container on the counter. She'll decide to eat a lemon crumb muffin. Eating a lemon crumb muffin will make her thirsty for a cup of tea. And chances are, if she gets herself a cup of tea, she'll want a minute to go with it.

LEMON CRUMB MUFFINS | BY TRISH BERG

Batter

1 cup butter (melted)	4 eggs	2 fresh lemons
2 cups sugar	⅜ teaspoon baking soda	Paper muffin cups
1 cup sour cream	1 tablespoon lemon juice	
3 cups flour	⅜ teaspoon salt	

Streusel

¾ cup sugar	¾ cup flour	¼ cup softened butter

Sift sugar and flour together. Add butter. Work into dry ingredients until crumbly.

Lemon Glaze

¼ cup sugar	⅙ cup lemon juice

Stir together until all of the sugar is dissolved.

Preheat oven to 350 degrees.

Batter: Mix all dry batter ingredients together and set aside. Grate rinds of lemons and set aside. In a separate bowl, mix eggs and sour cream; add in butter and lemon juice and blend.

Fold lemon rinds into batter. Add all dry ingredients into egg mixture. Blend well.

Place paper muffin cups in muffin tin. Fill each halfway with batter. Top each muffin with 1 tablespoon streusel. Bake for 18 to 20 minutes until cooked through.

Remove muffins from oven. Poke each several times with a toothpick and drizzle top of each muffin with some of the lemon glaze.

Yields: 12-24 muffins

You Might Be a Mommy If . . .

- You discuss your infant's bodily functions with strangers at the checkout.
- You can change a diaper quicker than a rodeo cowboy can rope a calf and wonder how you can apply that skill in the real world.
- Someone offered you five hundred dollars or an uninterrupted nap on a soft pillow, and you would choose the nap.
- You get excited when Pampers go on sale.
- Bedtime stories and goodnight prayers last longer than a light opera.

It's a Boy! And Another Boy!

BY KAREN ROBBINS

I sat in a rocking chair, surveying little ones on all fours around me. Belonging to a young church, our nursery bustled with new arrivals. In about two and a half months, I would add to that growing population. Since this was our first baby, the nursery committee decided I should get some practical experience before our little one came along. So I pulled nursery duty every couple of weeks while I was pregnant.

What I saw in that nursery appalled me. Kids sported crusty noses, matted hair, and dirty knees. When they weren't changed often enough, the diaper sometimes leaked indescribable fluids. I decided right then and there that *my* child would not look like any of these. I would keep him or her in tip-top shape, wiping that leaky nose often and keeping those knees clean. And the diaper would never overflow.

Then shortly before my due date, the doctor examined me and declared, "I feel a second head!"

Oh, great, I thought, a two-headed baby. Now what do we do?

Five days later, I went into labor early, and we discovered the second head actually belonged to a second baby. Twins!

During the next three months, I barely knew the time of day. My mother and mother-in-law lived three states away, and each spent a couple of weeks with me. However, even with the extra help, I mixed a never-ending lineup of formula, filled bottles, fed babies, washed clothes, and changed and bathed my two little boys. Left on my own, I felt lucky to get dressed before noon.

Things began to settle down a bit as I established a routine. Plus, having a little more time between feedings gave me the opportunity to catch my breath. I thought back to the time in the nursery when I had been critical of the other mothers. God must have looked down and chuckled as he formulated a plan: "Let's give her twins and see how she does."

My boys, Rob and Ron, fit into the nursery population quite well—crusty noses and all.

• Mommy's Little Helps •

TIMESAVING TIPS

CATHY
Train your family to use trash cans. First, equip each room in your home with an appropriate size trash can or waste basket. I've found that my family will not leave Band-Aid wrappers on the bathroom countertop if a trash basket is nearby. My automobile remained tidy because I kept a trash can designated for it in my garage. This saves time in re-collecting trash, and it makes trash day a breeze.

TRISH
Cook in bulk and swap meals with a friend or two a few nights a week. Supper swapping will save you time and money.

LESLIE
Develop a grocery list that matches the layout of your favorite store. Using a template I found online, I completed mine in about an hour. I print it out and put it on the fridge each week. My husband and kids circle what they need.

KAREN
Worrying over what's for dinner wastes time. Plan your meals a week at a time. Save menus as a quick reference for busy weeks.

TERRA
I wasted so much time dealing with mail—looking at it and setting it aside to act on later. Now I deal with each piece of mail as soon as it arrives at our house. When I receive a bill, I write a check at that moment and mail it the next day. This saves me time because I don't need to look for the bill at a later date. The goal is to touch each piece of mail only once.

24

CHAPTER TWO

Magic

Mama Sez

Sacrificial love knows no boundaries.

—CATHY MESSECAR

Nourishment for Mom's Spirit

Mary treasured up all these things . . . in her heart.

LUKE 2:19

FAMILY SNAPSHOT

Baby Names

BY TERRA HANGEN

Many parents experience great joy in finding the perfect name for a new baby. Will they use a solid, traditional name, a family name, or an unusual

25

name? When my parents expected their first baby, they decided on Terra for a girl and Colt for a boy. So I was named Terra, which means "earth" in Latin.

Sometimes a given name doesn't suit a person—my sister falls into that category. When she reached adulthood, Cindy changed her name to Sky. Now we sisters are earth and sky.

When my sons were born, the most popular names began with the letter J. But my husband and I also wanted to honor my parents, so we chose to name our first son Colt Joseph. When we named our second son Lane Christopher, it meant he shared the same middle name of his paternal grandfather. And thus, we named a new generation.

Before we had children, Will and I jokingly came up with two kids' names: Captain Energy for a boy and Synergy Moondance for a girl. While my sister and I enjoy our unusual names and their meanings, my sons should be eternally grateful that they are not Energy and Synergy. I think I will remind them of that—often.

MOM MISCELLANY

BY LESLIE WILSON

Unisex names are trending these days. American culture has moved from Frank, Harriet, Reginald, Beatrice, and Madge to Cameron, Taylor, Morgan, Chandler, and Casey. Will gender-specific names ever cycle back, or are names like Ernest, Alma, Roger, and Ethel gone forever? I love to think about the generations to come being called Aunt Sienna, Uncle Dakota, or—even worse—Grandma Katelyn and Grandpa Dylan.

But by the time it gets here, we'll probably be used to it.

A Few of Our Favorite Things

MOTHER'S DAY MEMORY

KAREN

When I dressed for church, I put on the handmade pierced earrings
my daughter had fashioned from clay, and my earlobes practically rested
on my shoulders from the weight. I proudly wore them all day.

TERRA

One year, I received a big bouquet of sunshine-yellow dandelions, carefully
picked by my elementary school age sons from a nearby park. The boys
presented them to me with love because they "knew Mom loves flowers."

TRISH

Riley drew a picture of the two of us together, holding hands. Our little
stick figures had curly hair and big smiles. And it said, "I love my mom
because she makes me smile." I keep that tucked in my Bible.

CATHY

When my son Russell was about four years old, he spied a water moccasin
on our sidewalk. Fear-stricken, he ran back into the house to tell me.
I quickly dispatched the poisonous snake to the netherworld, much to my
son's relief. In fifth grade, he made a construction paper card declaring on
the front "HAPPY MAMA'S DAY." Inside, the inscription said, "Thank You
For Killing the Snake When I Was Four Years Old!" In one corner, he had drawn
a huge star and awarded me a "GOLD STAR SPORT." A water leak destroyed
that precious card, but in my mind's eye, I can still see it three decades later.

LESLIE

My firstborn, Charlie, was ten months old for my first, official, he's-now-outside-the-womb Mother's Day. He'd learned a few words, but his favorite thing to say was "ya-ya-ya-ya-ya." Hubby Bret bought me a single rose—even that stretched our budget—and wrote the attached card on behalf of our young son: "To the best mommy in the whole, wide world. Ya-ya-ya-ya-ya! I love you! Charlie." Sorry, but I have to include one more favorite Mother's Day memory. At eight years old, my daughter, Molly, laid out a red carpet—made from every red towel in our house—stretching from my bedroom to the kitchen where she had a pancake breakfast waiting for me.

MOM MISCELLANY
SOUS CHEFS

By Cathy Messecar

A young child can help you chop boiled eggs or separate canned tuna or chicken chunks if you place the ingredients in a plastic or stainless steel bowl and give him or her a pastry cutter. Just toss peeled eggs into the bowl, and a child can easily press the pastry cutter into the eggs, chopping them into small pieces.

Mama Sez

A mother's arms are made of tenderness and children sleep soundly in them.

—Victor Hugo

• Mommy's Little Helps •
MONEY-SAVING TIPS

LESLIE
Limit your retail clothing choices. As quickly as kids grow from infancy to school age, they seem to need new outfits (and shoes!) every couple of months. Instead, scour garage sales, Craigslist, and resale shops. Frequent discount stores like Ross and TJ Maxx. Shop off-season—buy shorts when they're on sale for three dollars a pair. Ask friends to sell (or give) you their kids' hand-me-downs.

KAREN
Organize a fun party with friends where you can swap kids' clothes or Halloween costumes.

TERRA
Front-loading washers save money because they use much less water—meaning you pay for less water and less power to heat the water. Ask your local power company and municipal water department if they have rebate programs for buying water-saving clothes washers. We got two rebates on ours. Since there is no central agitator in a front-load washer, the clothes are treated more gently, and you can fit more clothes in one load. Most front-loading washers save a hundred dollars a year or more in water and energy costs.

TRISH
I just started using e-mealz (https://e-mealz.com) to save money on meal planning and grocery shopping. It costs five dollars per month, but for that small fee, you get seven weekly dinner menus, with recipes and corresponding grocery shopping lists all based on sales at your chosen grocery store. So far, I love it!

CATHY

My daughter went into a Goodwill store, her preteen son a reluctant tag-along. Since he now earns money from mowing yards, he buys some of his own clothes. Still, he had a hard time getting over the stigma of shopping at Goodwill. He was amazed to find brand-name jeans, like new (translation: faded), for as little as five dollars. Excited, he bought several pairs. Moms, let your children see you browse sale racks and resale shops, and your frugality might affect your clothing budget even more.

Adopting Love

By Karen Robbins

My husband, Bob, and I hoped to have both sons and daughters. So, after twins and a single birth resulted in all boys, we decided to begin an adoption search for a girl. With sons ages twelve and nine, I knew I didn't want a baby. We found an adoption agency that worked with hard-to-place older children and began the orientation program.

Once through the program and the home study, the agency asked us to consider several sibling groups and invited us to view a video of a sister and brother available for adoption. Watching the small television screen, my heart began to stir as I watched a beautiful little red-headed girl play with her younger brother. At six and five, they would fit perfectly with the boys' ages.

We arranged to meet them. Don couldn't stop smiling. Though a little hard to understand with his delayed speech development, he proudly shared his toy cars with us. Cheryl clung to her foster mom, but at the mention of McDonald's burgers and fries, both kids got excited. After that great first meeting, we eagerly planned for our boys to meet their prospective brother and sister.

The foster family invited us to a backyard BBQ so the kids could play together. Our boys developed a rapport with Don almost instantly because they could do all the young male bonding things—play with Hot Wheels, throw and catch a ball, and so on. But my sons had no idea what to do with Cheryl.

She and I played together, running in the grass and kicking a ball. I fell to the ground giggling and suddenly found Cheryl on top of me. She sat on my stomach and peered at me, her crystal blue eyes boring into mine as if she saw the depths of my soul. Just as quickly, she hopped up and ran off again. Whatever transpired in those few moments still mystifies me.

The idea of having a new little brother and sister excited my boys. We talked about it all the way home.

"Just think," I said to Andy. "You won't be the baby anymore."

Silence. I turned in my seat to see if one of the twins had a hand over his mouth. Andy studied his shoes.

"It's nice to be the baby in the family," he whispered.

Wow, I thought. What do I do now?

"Andy, you will always be my *baby*. Don will be my *little one*." Inwardly, I thanked God for his instant wisdom. Andy brightened and the chatter continued.

Over the next two months, we gradually included Cheryl and Don in our family. A couple of weekend stays, then a week, then Placement Day—the day they would come to stay.

Excitement and expectations grew as the date neared. I felt certain that having them in our home all the time—and getting into a routine—would meld us magically as a family. But magic is something found only in story books.

Placement Day followed by Adoption Day launched me into an adventure in motherhood like no other. With God's grace we all survived each other.

I'm often asked if I love my biological children more than my adopted children. No. I love each child differently. Each possesses a unique personality and deserves to be loved for who he or she is—not how I became his or her mother.

You Might Be a Mommy If . . .

- Your alarm clock is your child's face two inches from your own asking what's for breakfast.
- The ER staff knows you by name.
- Weary is written on your face, but happy is written on your heart.
- You spend more on babysitters than you do on your utilities.
- You've memorized the number to the pediatrician's office, but you can't remember your own cell phone number.
- You have to tuck in your tummy before you tuck in your blouse.

Nourishment for Mom's Spirit

For you created my inmost being; you knit me together in my mother's womb.

PSALM 139:13

Milk Machine

By Leslie Wilson

Melanie and I sat on the bed and floor, respectively, intent on watching our friend—a mom of newborn twins—breastfeed both babies at the same time. Debbie assumed her position on the bed and placed a giant wraparound foam pillow across her lap.

"I have to take off my whole top or the kids can't breathe," she explained, lifting her faded T-shirt over her head. "It's impossible to do this with any kind of modesty." As though we needed an explanation.

She placed Kristin at one breast, Caleb at the other. The babies rooted around momentarily, then began to suck greedily, occasionally squirming this way or that.

Just when it began to look as though Debbie's efforts might be successful, her husband, Alex, walked in.

Okay, picture this with me—once again.

Half-naked wife rests on the king-sized bed with a child at each breast. Two of her female friends sit within spitting distance.

The unbelievable part: Alex didn't run right back out of the room. Nor did he immediately head to the bathroom—where he apparently needed to get something. Otherwise, there was no logical reason for him to enter the room.

No. Alex decided to invite even more humiliation and discomfort into what was already an embarrassing situation.

Get this—Dear Old Dad walked right over to the bed and gazed adoringly at his wife.

Already on the verge of cracking up, Melanie and I couldn't help but look. We knew we shouldn't, but something continued to draw us in. Like curiously sick patrons at a carnival freak show, our rubbernecking lacked subtlety.

And then he spoke.

"They're beautiful, aren't they?" he said, trance-like.

Short pause. Then . . . I could no longer remain silent. (Sorry, gang, for my lack of self-control. I just couldn't help myself.)

"Oh, you mean the babies," I said, alternately pointing from new mom to babies and back.

Alex, getting my joke, finally found his feet and scurried back into the living room. The rest of us enjoyed one of our best laughs ever—completely at his expense. Occasionally, I still feel uncomfortable *for* him.

A Few of Our Favorite Things
BOOK OR BEDTIME STORY

TERRA
The favorite story in our home is *The Runaway Bunny* with text by Margaret Wise Brown and pictures by Clement Hurd. The author charmingly shows that a mother's love is endless and strong and that we protect our little ones. In this book for ages two to six, a baby bunny says he is going to run away, and his mother shows how she will find him and keep him safe. For example, he says he will become a bird and fly away, and the mother bunny says she will become a tree to be his home.

TRISH
Some of our best bedtime stories shared while we snuggled under the blankets include *Goodnight Moon* by Margaret Wise Brown, *Where the Wild Things Are* by Maurice Sendak, and the *Little House on the Prairie* series by Laura Ingalls Wilder. We also enjoyed the *American Girl* books.

LESLIE
Like Trish's family, my kids grew up on Laura Ingalls's adventures. My husband also read *The Chronicles of Narnia* aloud to our children—twice. Of the preschool books, we particularly like If *You Give a Mouse a Cookie* by Laura Joffe Numeroff, illustrated by Felicia Bond.

CATHY
Elbert's Bad Word by Audrey Wood and illustrated by Audrey and Don Wood tells a charming story about a young boy who "caught" a bad word at an adult party one afternoon, and he snatched it from the air and stuffed it in his pocket. When a croquet mallet later lands on poor Elbert's great toe, out springs the bad word, "uglier and bigger than before." He manages to get rid of the bad

word with the help of his mother and a gardener-wizard. He learned to use strong words when needed, but not bad words.

KAREN

Dr. Seuss books have always been my favorites. I also quietly sang my favorite hymn, "In the Garden," as a lullaby.

40

CHAPTER THREE

Adventure

Mama Sez

Seek the counsel of grandmothers. They earned their gray hair.

—CATHY MESSECAR

FAMILY SNAPSHOT

What No Mom Ever Tells You

BY TRISH BERG

Motherhood is a wild adventure, and we moms can learn many life lessons from each other. After all, who better to prepare you for what lies ahead than another mom who's been where you are now?

During my first pregnancy, moms advised me on how to eat. I listened to moms tell me to get the epidural during labor and other moms tell me to have my baby the "natural" way, with no medication. Some moms told me to have the baby sleep in my room in a bassinet; others said to use the crib from day one.

Advice came from all sides, and suddenly every decision overwhelmed me. It seemed like every mom I knew had the best way to do something, and boy did they want to share it with me.

But no mom ever told me that nursing your baby could be hard.

The first time they laid Hannah in my arms, I began to nurse her. What should have been a precious and tender moment wasn't. It hurt. There, I said it. It hurt much more than I expected it to.

About four months later, I suffered a breast infection. That pain felt worse than being in labor, fully dilated with no epidural. Add a fever and chills on top of that, and I was miserable.

When Hannah weaned herself at about eleven months old, I cried. How could she choose a bottle over me?

As a veteran mom who has nursed four babies through their first year, I will be the first one to tell you not to stress about nursing. It's a wonderful thing if you can do it. But if you choose to bottle feed, or nursing doesn't work for you, don't worry. Your child will be fed either way with nourishment and love from the one God chose to be his mom.

. . Word Quilters' Wisdom . .

THE BEDTIME ROUTINE

TRISH

When our toddlers and preschoolers had nightmares and came into our bedroom at night, we had them sleep on the floor next to our bed, snuggled with their blanket and pillow. They felt safe, and we slept better without their feet in our backs.

CATHY

If children have plenty of physical activity throughout the day, they're more likely to rest well at night. Establish a routine that includes about thirty minutes of quiet time before going to bed (no television, limited noise in household). Allow them to wear comfortable sleepwear (cotton T-shirt and undies). Provide a very soft light to ease them into slumber.

KAREN

Sometimes, no matter how good your bedtime routine, it just doesn't work. When our boys—like so many other children—went through that difficult time where they wouldn't stay in bed, I shed many tears and said many prayers. I found that prayers are answered and tears are cleansing.

TERRA

To encourage a child to sleep in his own bed, set up a routine that he likes. You could give him a hot bath, let him pick out favorite stuffed animals, and drink a glass of milk. When he is in bed, read him a story, say a prayer, give hugs and kisses, and say goodnight. Keep to the routine so all the steps to sleep are there with no surprises.

LESLIE

Make their room a wonderful place to be. Talk about them sleeping in their own bed—when they're not in bed. Praise them for staying in bed. Use Terra's hint about developing an effective bedtime routine. Then accept that sometimes kids need to cry it out. I know I do. Why do we feel the need to always rescue ourselves—and our children—from God-given emotion?

Bath Time

By Leslie Wilson

While pregnant, I envisioned my baby's bath time would be a tender moment with soothing songs and cascading water. Think Johnson's Baby Shampoo commercials with the wide-eyed baby laughing and clapping as his mother gently and carefully rinses the No More Tears formula out of her child's downy locks, never once getting water or suds in her little one's eyes.

You might think it took a few months or years for me to sour on bathing my children. Nope. Happened on the first try. Yep. In the giant, blue, plastic infant bathtub I placed on the kitchen counter for Charlie's inaugural cleansing.

Okay, in my defense (have you ever noticed when people say "in my defense" that the stuff to follow ain't so great for their victim, which in this case was my three-day-old son?), I gave birth to Charlie at five o'clock on a Friday afternoon. Baylor University Medical Center didn't offer the neonatal care classes over the weekend. Apparently, if I wanted to know how to breastfeed, burp, diaper, or bathe my child, I should have delivered him on a weekday. Anyway, Bret and I left the hospital with no hands-on training. My working knowledge came straight from *What to Expect When You're Expecting* and my field experience from my little sister, eight years younger. Truth is, I would have felt more comfortable sporting the latest swimwear styles in a crowded mall, with my post-pregnancy body.

I filled the bathtub with warm water. Or, to be completely accurate, what felt *to me* like warm water. After all, my baby's tender skin would be exposed in the cool air of our tiny kitchen. I didn't want him to be too cold. Then, I placed Charlie into the water only to hear his piercing scream that could be heard in three counties. His skin turned bright red. Lobsters in a pot had nothing on this kid!

Bret rushed in from the bedroom. "What in the world's going on?"

"I'm just giving Charlie a bath." I poured cup after cup of water over him in an effort to soothe his cries. "But he doesn't seem to like it."

"I'd say he hates it. Get him out of there," the equally new father insisted, grabbing the hooded infant towel from the kitchen table.

As soon as Bret touched the water, he recoiled. "Um, honey, I think I know why Charlie was crying. You've practically scalded him."

"What?"

"This water is burning me, so I can only imagine how it feels to his tender skin."

"Really? I just wanted it to be warm enough."

"Well, I think you got it a little too warm." Bret wrapped the towel loosely around little Charlie and held him close. "Why don't you add some cooler water? I bet he'll like it then."

After Bret talked me down off the ledge, and I stopped sobbing uncontrollably about the near-scalding of my precious young son, I cooled the water and gently placed Charlie back into the tub. Though he didn't exactly laugh and coo—remember he was less than a week old—he didn't cry and even seemed to enjoy himself a little bit.

Not long after this incident, Bret took over giving Charlie his bath. He subsequently bathed our other children as well, which incidentally worked out quite nicely for me. (Now ladies, you did not hear me say scalding your child will get you out of bathing duty.)

The whole bath issue came full circle when Charlie, at seventeen, scolded me for rinsing dinner dishes while he showered in the nearby downstairs bath as he got ready for a date. "Mom, you nearly scalded me every time you turned on and off the water."

I smiled. If he only knew.

You Might Be a Mommy If . . .

- Baby wipes are the equivalent of the American Express card—you don't leave home without them.
- You voluntarily expose your breasts in public, and no one is paying you to.
- You mastered the skill of speed showering and wonder if a world record could be in the works.
- Your child throws up, and you actually try to catch it in your hands.
- You started watching *Survivor* thinking it would be autobiographical.
- You sleep with a baby monitor a foot away from your head.
- You carry a diaper bag instead of a purse.
- You have spit-up near the shoulder of every shirt you own.

MOM MISCELLANY
THE BEST BABY BOOK

By Terra Hangen

My parents and my husband's parents made baby scrapbooks for us, and my husband and I continued that tradition with our sons. We included all the usual stuff: weight and length at birth, date and place of birth, a lock of baby's hair, first time to laugh, first word spoken, first time to stand up, and other sweet milestones of a new life.

For our sons' books, I inserted pictures behind the plastic of blank photo albums. I typed up information and stories to insert among the photos, birth announcements, and locks of hair.

What makes a baby memory scrapbook sparkle is adding anecdotes to it. My sons like where I added stories about when they went to the circus and ate cotton candy, which became a sticky tasty mess, or how our two-year-old rode his tricycle into the swimming pool and kept pedaling at the bottom of the pool, until Dad pulled him out, still pedaling. (Yes, we stood right there and watched him ride into the pool. Caught completely off-guard, it took us a second to react.) Thankfully, our son didn't even cry. He just got back on his bike.

If you put together a baby memory book, make sure it has the elements in it that you want. If you're like me and want to include information on siblings and extended family, look for those features. Moms today can find pages online and download them to take to a print shop to be printed on fancy paper. There are also companies that let you create a book online, and they will mail you a printed copy.

Just remember to add stories of some funny family moments and dramatic events so you will enjoy reading it together in the days and years ahead.

Mom to Mom

By Trish Berg

When my first baby arrived, I desperately needed advice. Okay. Every day of my life I need advice, especially on mothering. When we brought Hannah home from the hospital, a parade of family and friends greeted us. They all wanted to hold our new baby girl (which totally freaked me out, by the way). They all had suggestions on how I could be a great mom. At least they brought us food, which meant I usually let them in the door, despite my new mom germ-paranoia.

Everybody had a piece of advice, and I tried desperately to soak it all in:

- Sleep when the baby sleeps.
- Don't worry about the laundry.
- Only feed her every two hours.
- Feed her whenever she cries.
- Don't use a pacifier to calm her.
- Pacifiers are the best.
- Put her on your schedule; don't adapt to hers.
- Put her on her back to sleep.
- Put her on her side to sleep.
- Make sure to burp her upright.
- Hold her head.
- Protect her soft spot.

- Swaddle her this way.
- Diaper her that way.
- And whatever you do, don't take her in public for at least three months.

Like a whirlwind rushing through my mind and my home, the advice came in and swept my sanity away. Well, maybe the lack of sleep did that. Either way, I was a nervous wreck most of the time that first year—trying to do everything right, usually doing it all wrong.

But when it came down to it, mothering was as simple as 1-2-3.

Love your kids.

Pray for them.

Commit yourself to mothering them.

Spend time with them. And when you do make a mistake, apologize to them, ask their forgiveness, and strive to do better tomorrow.

Stop worrying about everything that is going wrong, and try to remember that no mom is perfect. Don't be afraid to ask for help or advice when you need it.

A Few of Our Favorite Things
COOKBOOKS

CATHY
A kitchen sign reads, "My collection of cookbooks is far superior
to my cooking." In my last move, I got rid of many cookbooks, but the one
I plan to keep the longest is *The Illustrated Encyclopedia of American Cooking*,
my 1987 edition. A friend told me about a chocolate cake his mother used to
make that had sauerkraut in it, and he said, "I'd love to have the recipe." You
guessed it: I looked in my cookbook, and there it was. I even baked it for him.
It's not my favorite recipe, but I'm sure it held fond memories from his boyhood.

TERRA
My favorite cookbook is the tried-and-true *Joy of Cooking* by Irma S. Rombauer.
Its best feature is that it includes very basic things like how to hard boil an egg.
Don't laugh. I needed that instruction. In more than eight hundred pages,
the author covers every recipe you could want. My current edition is so
well-used that someday I vow to buy a new one and then spend hours
copying my handwritten notes from the old copy into the new one.

TRISH
Betty Crocker's Cookbook/40th Anniversary Edition—There's nothing like a classic.
I look up everything from measuring equivalents to how to make the best pie crust.

LESLIE
Working Woman's Cookbook—Co-workers, paralegals, and assistants at my workplace
compiled favorite family recipes into a cookbook for us all to have as a keepsake.
Imagine my surprise when my dad added the parenthetical "With Strong Stomachs"
between Woman's and Cookbook in the title! I laugh every time I look at that cover. In

addition to those in the cookbook, I've taped dozens of extra recipes in the margins. I can truly say that cookbook is one of a kind.

KAREN
Betty Crocker's Cookbook for Kids—My adopted grandma gave me this cookbook when I was nine. It puts clever recipes into very simple terms for kids—or people like me—who are still learning to cook.

CHAPTER FOUR

Memories

Mama Sez

Never wake a sleeping baby.

—EVERY MOM

FAMILY SNAPSHOT

First Toddler Steps

BY CATHY MESSECAR

When I found out I was pregnant with our first child, my husband, David, and I told family members individually when we next saw them. We lived on his grandmother's farm, renting an older house from her. A widow for many years and a kind woman, she was nevertheless determined to have her own way about most things. So, when my husband and I told her we were going to have a baby—her first great-grandchild, she energetically shook her arthritic finger in my face and said, "You *must* have a boy first."

I shook in my western boots, knowing that despite her wants, the sex of our firstborn was already determined. She had only one child, a son, who had passed down the family name to my husband. And it seemed family pride demanded that we should have a son to do the same. Much to her delight, about seven and a half months later, I followed orders and delivered a boy. We even named our son Russell, after her late husband.

She doted on him. But then one day at her house, as he crawled on the floor, Great Grandma asked in an authoritative voice, "Is he walking yet?"

He had not yet taken steps alone. At eleven months, he showed some interest. However, up to this time, he had only held on to tables or performed the "monkey walk"—where a beginner takes practice steps with both arms anchored to an adult's hands. Timidly, I admitted, "He holds on to tables and walks around them, but he hasn't taken any steps by himself."

Great Grandmother reached for a bear-in-a-cage rolling toy. She held it out to Russell, who was on the opposite side of the room. That's when Russell decided to take his debut steps and make a fibber out of his mom. He turned loose of the table and walked ten steps by himself, straight into his great-grandmother's arms. "Why see there," she declared. "He *can* walk."

Very appropriate that this matriarch should coax his little legs to take their first steps. After all, she'd dictated that he would be a boy and carry on the family name. I guess she could tell him when to start walking, too.

Word Quilters' Wisdom

WAYS TO CALM KIDS

TERRA

When children near two years of age, they may lie down on the floor and kick and scream. If this happens at home, you may find it best to ignore the tantrum. When your child calms down, you can reward the calm by suggesting, "Let's finger paint," or "Let's do this puzzle." Simply let the tantrum fizzle out. When calm returns, direct your child to an activity you both like. My best advice on tantrums is don't let your child control your actions and get what he or she wants by throwing a fit. If your child has a tantrum in public, remove him or her from the watchful eyes of onlookers, and allow the child to calm down before returning to the store or restaurant.

LESLIE

Have children practice self-control—sit cross-legged with hands in laps and breathe deeply, in and out—when you're not in a stressful or panicked situation. That way, when kids flirt with a tantrum or just get upset by something, they'll know how to calm themselves. Also, model calm behavior for them.

KAREN

Music helps to soothe the soul. Choose wisely.

CATHY

Sing a merry tune, softly or loudly. Act your silliest. Dance with a broom. Start a pretend conversation with the television, pet canary, your foot, or the sofa cushion. Do something extremely out of the ordinary, and your child's frantic mood may relax and turn to giggles within minutes.

TRISH

Focus kids on a joint task. From toddlers to teenagers, when my children argue or fight, I redirect them to complete a task together. Making them work as a team to accomplish something (like cleaning the basement) makes them forget their fight altogether.

Charlie's First Birthday

By Leslie Wilson

*O*ur oldest son's first birthday party seems dull by today's standards. The attendee list was short—just Birthday Boy Charlie, his maternal grandparents, G.G. (his great-grandma on my dad's side), Bret, and me. We hadn't planned any festivities or games, though I had baked a somewhat lopsided chocolate birthday cake. But when Charlie tasted it, he made an awful face. Apparently, he didn't share the love for All Things Chocolate that his mom did. I rushed to take a bite myself, wondering if I'd left out the sugar or absentmindedly added Tabasco or something equally disgusting. The chocolaty goodness tickled my taste buds and slid down my throat. Then it hit me! My young son had never eaten dessert; the only sugar he'd had up to that point was hidden in baby food like peaches and plums.

G.G. placed a bowl of green beans in front of him. She'd been snapping them (removing the ends before cooking), which had captured his interest. As he munched on several, his happy face returned.

Charlie clapped his hands and tried to chime in as we sang "Happy Birthday" to him. Bret helped him blow out the candles. But once that excitement ended, he went back to chomping green beans. The rest of us forced ourselves to enjoy the chocolate cake on his behalf.

My parents had driven down from Colorado for the occasion, and we visited with them about everything that had happened since their last trip to Texas. That led to us counting up the number of trips they'd made since Charlie's birth. Twelve total—an average of one a month! My husband shocked me when he announced suddenly, "If y'all have made that many trips down here in a year, you should just move here."

Famous last words.

Within two months, my dad had applied for and received a transfer within his company. They sold their home, rented a place in a Dallas suburb, and moved to Texas.

I couldn't think of a better first birthday gift for their grandson.

You Might Be a Mommy If . . .

- With each subsequent child, you've progressed from sterilizing the pacifier to washing it off to blowing on it, invoking the three-second rule.
- You wash fourteen loads of laundry every week, and your one child is only three months old.
- You have the number for poison control on speed dial.
- In order to cuddle with your husband, you'd have to crawl over a dog, two kids, fourteen stuffed animals, and a pile of clean laundry.
- A good day means getting dressed *and* making dinner.
- You've read *Goodnight Moon* 487 times—this week!
- You hum "Brahms's Lullaby" absentmindedly.
- You keep five sizes of clothes in your closet.
- You can pee with three children watching you—and only two are yours.

Mama Sez

Who ran to help me when I fell,
And would some pretty story tell,
Or kiss the place to make it well?
My mother.

—Ann Taylor

First Haircut

By Cathy Messecar

Though not even a year old, Russell already owned jeans and boots. Ready or not, Mama, boyhood knocked. For a few weeks, my husband had suggested, "Don't you think it's time for his first haircut?" The blond, curly hair resting on the collar of my son's shirt made him look like such a baby. I knew it was time, but I hesitated having those adorable wheat-colored curls chopped off.

Finally, I gave in. We trekked to the barber about an hour before closing time on a Saturday afternoon. My baby usually wore one-piece outfits with snaps in the crotch for easy diaper changes, but for this momentous occasion, I chose his jeans, boots, and a striped T-shirt in autumn colors.

Babies respond differently when exposed to new experiences—from awe to terror, with a range of emotions in between. I'd seen dads sit with their eight-month-old sons in their laps to calm the child for his first trim. However, we expected that our rather laid-back baby would tolerate his new haircut with calm.

The personable barber, Mr. Percy, made his brand-new customer right at home. He showed Russell his shears and turned them on so he could hear the buzzing sound they made. He also had toys, including an especially annoying rubber ducky that when squeezed made a high-pitched quack. Though Russell had weighed over nine pounds at birth, he looked small sitting in that big, old barber chair. Always rated in the upper percentile of height and weight charts, he managed to look quite the infant sitting under the massive, striped drape designed to keep clipped hairs from showering him.

At home, my active baby remained motionless only when he was asleep. But sitting atop the barber's specially made, padded seat that rested across the arms of the big barber chair, my son didn't move an inch. The barber switched on the shears, and baby Russell never flinched. He just kept staring ahead at my husband and me, seated right in front of him.

Ever the mommy, I brought a white envelope with me, and when the first curl hit the floor, I rushed to scoop it up and save it. For what, I wasn't sure, but my mother had saved a lock of my hair, and I wanted a strand of my son's.

Within minutes, the barber finished cutting his hair. Mr. Percy dipped a softly bristled brush in powder and whisked off the back of Russell's neatly trimmed new hairline. He even put a tiny dab of masculine aftershave on his thumb and christened the crown of my baby's head. He gently removed the drape and said, "All done, young man." His pronounced words seemed a hocus pocus, an abracadabra, and an open sesame. My baby transformed into a boy in only a few ticks of the clock.

The moment my son jumped into the car, he returned to his typical, rowdy self. Almost as if he knew he had traversed a passageway, he jumped and planted both feet firmly on the car seat. When we got home, he bounced on the hardwood floors, romped, and played rough with his toys. The Tonka trucks didn't quietly "putt putt" anymore. They roared.

Perhaps curls belong to babies and girls. How could I, a first-time mother, know that snipping off lovable springy tresses would release the little boy inside my son?

Consider this a fair warning, young mother: A first haircut may magically turn baby fat into little boy spunk.

A Few of Our Favorite Things
FAMILY TRADITIONS

TRISH
Every Sunday night, I make homemade pizza and we watch a
movie together. The kids look forward to that all week long.

KAREN
Dinner was always at six as my kids were growing up. Attendance was expected.

TERRA
The words "let's do a mixed grill tonight" bring the response of "Yes!"
from all who hear it at our house. My husband, Will, cooks an assortment
of salmon, steak, shrimp, bratwurst, sliced zucchini, and eggplant on the grill.
Add a tossed salad and corn on the cob, and dinner is served.

LESLIE
I require my family to go over the calendar every week after Sunday
dinner (at noon). Everybody grouses about it, but we end up having some
of our best conversations during this time. Plus, it helps teach my kids to be
more organized with their schedules! (Don't tell anyone, but it wouldn't surprise
me if my kids establish this tradition with their own families someday.)

CATHY
We made up a more exciting version of the "I Spy" game that Dad, Mom,
and kids enjoyed playing when we drove to town (a thirty-minute drive) or took
longer trips. We each took turns naming items, animals, or activities we were likely
to see on a particular road. In the summer, a suggestion might be, "Find someone
mowing a lawn." The first to spy the named object or activity won the game and
received the honor of choosing what our family would next search for.

MOM MISCELLANY

By Terra Hangen

If your kids are tired of sandwiches and chips in school lunch bags, ask them what they would like, and then plan to shop together for ingredients. My children loved bagels with cream cheese and California sushi rolls. To keep the lunch cool, freeze a juice box and put the lunch and juice in an insulated bag.

CHAPTER FIVE

Prayers

Mama Sez

I remember my mother's prayers and they have always followed me.
They have clung to me all my life.

—ABRAHAM LINCOLN

FAMILY SNAPSHOT

A Little Help Here, Mom

BY KAREN ROBBINS

When it came time for our son Andy to start preschool, I wasn't worried about the must-be-potty-trained rule. At age three, Andy was *good*. He knew exactly when nature called and made it to the potty with enough time to spare. I credited my experience in training his older twin brothers with the reason that Andy caught on so quickly. Instead of rushing him, I waited for him to be ready to train, even though the pediatrician had suggested I start him at an earlier age.

But the road to being a big boy was not without its bumps—namely, having to deal with all the buttons, snaps, and zippers on his pants.

I hosted the very first meeting of all the Cooperative Preschool moms. The landing on the upper level of our split-level home opened to the living room, which gave a good view of the kids' bathroom upstairs. As the meeting began, I happily noticed that Andy had not only gone potty, but he had also remembered to close the bathroom door. My bubble of pride deflated quickly, however, when my son waddled to the top of the stairs, his pants around his ankles, and asked, "Mom, can you help?"

This group of preschool moms who didn't know each other bonded suddenly as they shared in my embarrassment and we all had a good belly laugh. Talk about an icebreaker!

BEST ADVICE FROM MY MOM

TRISH

Give yourself a break. Aim for a C on your house cleaning or cooking
report card, and know that it will all be okay in the end. Crumbs
on the kitchen floor or Ramen Noodles for supper never killed anyone.

TERRA

The best advice I ever got from my mom about parenting was to make sure
that my family attends church and that the kids go to Sunday school. This
gives them a rich background that will stay with them throughout their lives.

CATHY

Verbally forgive your child for misbehaviors, and then make sure you never bring it up
again. That kind of parent-modeled forgiveness is the same kind we receive from God.

KAREN

Mom gave me the idea to recycle corduroy pants and jeans by making
cut-offs and using the cut-off parts to make quilts for the boys' bunks.

LESLIE

Holding my six-week-old firstborn son, I asked my mom why she had never shared
with me how hard it was to be a new mom—the lack of sleep, the mood swings, the
sheer physical exhaustion. Mom said, "Oh honey, you forget that part." At the
time, I doubted her words. Five, ten, twenty years later, I realize she was right.

A Few of Our Favorite Things

WEBSITES

LESLIE

Mothers of Preschoolers (www.mops.org) provides resources and community for mothers with specific needs, including those who work outside the home, have school-aged kids, stay at home with preschoolers, have kids with special needs, have multiples, have a child serving in the military, or had a child late in life. I'm also partial to this organization, having been a MOPS mom for seven years, a mentor mom for five, and a speaker at many groups.

CATHY

One of my favorite websites is Plugged In, at www.pluggedin.com, a product of Focus on the Family. I can read honest movie reviews there before I take my family. The reviews include exact information as to movie violence, sex, language, spiritual content, and much more. I've relied on it for years because movie trailers are designed to entice, and they do not necessarily reveal inappropriate content.

TERRA

Focus on the Family provides sound guidance on topics for parents of children of all ages at www.focusonthefamily.com/parenting. They share free information on topics including single parenting, adoptive families, parenting kids with special needs, kindergarten readiness, potty training, sleep issues, and more.

TRISH

Hybrid Her (www.hybridher.com) is all about the entrepreneurial mom—from celebrating the spirit and showcasing the goods to helping make the actual connections that lead to business.

KAREN

We thoroughly enjoy the websites that make picture books and calendars with our favorite pictures.

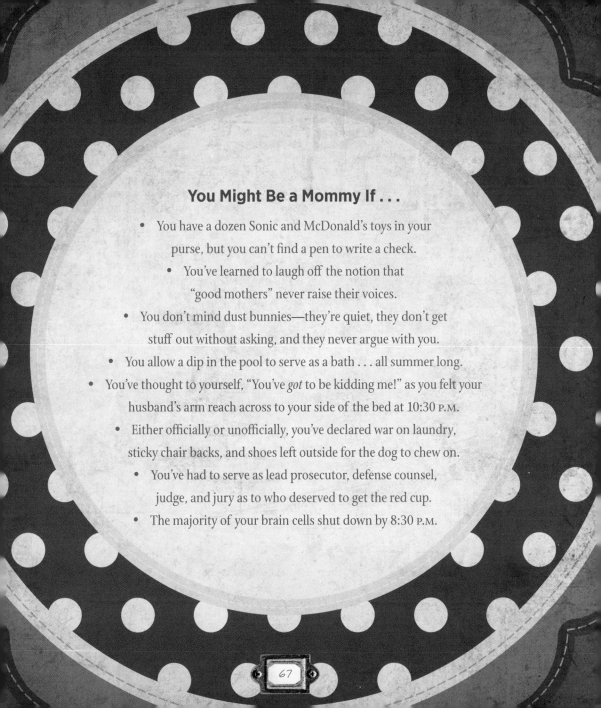

You Might Be a Mommy If . . .

- You have a dozen Sonic and McDonald's toys in your purse, but you can't find a pen to write a check.
- You've learned to laugh off the notion that "good mothers" never raise their voices.
- You don't mind dust bunnies—they're quiet, they don't get stuff out without asking, and they never argue with you.
- You allow a dip in the pool to serve as a bath . . . all summer long.
- You've thought to yourself, "You've *got* to be kidding me!" as you felt your husband's arm reach across to your side of the bed at 10:30 P.M.
- Either officially or unofficially, you've declared war on laundry, sticky chair backs, and shoes left outside for the dog to chew on.
- You've had to serve as lead prosecutor, defense counsel, judge, and jury as to who deserved to get the red cup.
- The majority of your brain cells shut down by 8:30 P.M.

Garden Children

By Terra Hangen

*A*re toads, earthworms, snakes, snails, weeds, and watering cans part of playtime at your house? I recall the fun my children had one sunny day when I found them digging in the dirt in our garden.

Garden children seem specially blessed. They have contact with bright colors, bird song, heavenly scents, and mud between their toes—all while enjoying the creativity of planting and nurturing green things.

Instead of saying to our two sons, "Go outside and play," I often said, "Let's go see what's in the garden." Colt and Lane began gardening as toddlers, and everything seemed new and miraculous to them. To plant a seed and see its tiny sprout a week later produces awe in little kids—and in their moms, too.

Our cats helped by napping nearby in the sun and watching my kids and neighbor kids plant sunflower seeds by poking their fingers in the soil, dropping in a seed, and patting soil to cover it. Our pet chickens, Tick and Tock, scratched in the dirt nearby. My kids chose which seeds to plant; top choices for them included sunflowers, zucchini, Chinese sugar peas, pumpkin, radish, and cucumbers.

We built a garden teepee using eight ten-foot-tall bamboo plant stakes, tied together at the top. We set the stakes six inches into the soil in a circle, leaving a small area for an entrance. At the base of each stake, our sons planted seeds of climbing vines. Our favorite teepee vine was the scarlet runner bean, which has edible beans and blazing crimson flowers that attract hummingbirds. We also planted sweet pea, moonflower, and nasturtium seeds, which grew into vines that covered the teepee and created a sacred place with "no grownups allowed" inside the sanctuary.

Moonflowers are beloved at our house since the flowers open only after sundown and seem to glow with a white light, making visits to the garden or teepee at night very mysterious.

One day as I knelt in our garden with my sons, weeding and planting, I jumped and jerked my hand back as a black snake hurried away from me. Colt and Lane thought the snake was great and yelled "gardener snake" as they tried to grab the snake, which was black with yellow racing stripes down each side. The snake slithered to a safe hiding place behind some giant chard plants, where we couldn't catch him. He lived in our garden all summer.

Could this digging in the mud and watching plants and wildlife lead to a career as a botanist or biologist or to a lifelong hobby of gardening? Only time and the gardener snake will tell.

Word Quilters' Wisdom

POTTY TRAINING—ADVICE FROM US ALL

Tossing a few Cheerios in the toilet helped the boys learn to aim better.

No matter when you start or what you do, your child will determine his own time to be trained. Have patience. Make the "big potty" available, but remember that pressuring kids makes everyone miserable!

Relax. It will happen in due time. We've never seen a college grad wearing a pull-up.

Be gentle and patient. You used to soil your underwear, and one day you might do so again.

Nourishment for Mom's Spirit

Build houses and settle down; plant gardens and eat what they produce.

JEREMIAH 29:5

You Might Be a Mommy If . . .

- You eat baby food—occasionally when there's no baby in the room.
- Your last hairstyle was in 1999.
- Sleeping in is when the clock reads 7:30.
- Digging out your kid's splinter ranks among the most painful moments of *your* life.
- You buy three gallons of milk and five boxes of cereal every time you go to the store.
- Getting away means taking a bubble bath.
- You've ever used tweezers to retrieve a LEGO (or raisin or aquarium rock or button or dime) out of your son's nose.
- You'll willingly hug and kiss a kid who has sticky fingers, sweat-drenched hair, and a milk mustache.

A Few of Our Favorite Things

FAMILY VACATION

KAREN

Our first vacation with five kids found us in the Smoky Mountains
fishing at a stocked trout pond. The five kids caught fish so quickly
that the kind attendant reminded me we had to pay by the pound.

TRISH

Family Church Camp at Camp Luther—We spend a week every summer
drawing closer to Christ when we stay in rustic cabins, eat in the dining
hall, and hang out with our children with no TV, no radio, no electronics.

LESLIE

Our family often visits Branson, Missouri, and stays in my parents' condo there.
We love the wholesome, family atmosphere—and there's no shortage of
wonderful activities and attractions (shows, amusements parks, water park,
miniature golf, zip line, helicopter rides, water skiing, House of Wax, Titanic exhibit,
Ripley's Believe It or Not, three [yes, **three**] outlet malls, hiking, boating, movie
theaters, golf, horseback riding). One day while walking around Silver Dollar City,
I asked my son, Charlie, what he thought would happen if Jesus were to return
at that exact moment. He looked around at the workers and patrons at the
amusement park and answered, "Well, there wouldn't be anybody here." So true!

TERRA

A favorite family vacation included soaking in Grover Hot Springs, which is outdoors in
California's Sierra Nevada Mountains. It is particularly fun to sit in the hot springs pool
while it's raining—and you can see flashes of lightning far away and heading closer.

CATHY

We didn't take extended vacations, since my husband and I were the only workers in our family business. However, we did travel short distances to nearby theme parks and attractions. Since we didn't have a swimming pool at home, on a couple of the hottest summer weekends, we'd check into a hotel about an hour's drive from our home and let the kids swim until they splashed all the water out of the pool! A fun mini-getaway.

74

CHAPTER SIX

Treasures

MOM MISCELLANY
JOB SECURITY

BY LESLIE WILSON

As a mom, I can sometimes fall into the trap of devaluing my job.

Lately, however, I've noticed a few things that could solidify my standing, my role within the family. If these items don't render me indispensable, I don't know what will.

Because . . . if I don't do these things, no one will:

- Remove lint from the dryer filter.
- Clean out the refrigerator.
- Change the bed sheets.
- Use coupons.
- Make any kind of powdered drink.
- Change the toilet paper roll.

I should never question my significance or my role in my family. I'm needed. I'm an integral part, a necessary cog. I may not keep everything moving, but I do have complete authority over a few aspects of household management.

Even if it's by default.

A mother is a person who, seeing there are only four pieces of pie for five people, promptly announces she never did care for pie.

—TENNEVA JORDAN

A Few of Our Favorite Things
KIDS SAY THE FUNNIEST THINGS

KAREN

My son mixed his grandmother's trip to Pennsylvania
with the memory verse he was trying to learn in Sunday school.
"Thou shalt not take the Lord's name to Pennsylvania!"

LESLIE

Reese: Mom, may I please have some Skittles?
Mom: Sure. Hey, we have ice cream if you'd rather have that.
Reese: No, I like Skittles.
Mom: Are you a Skittles connoisseur?
Reese: I don't know what that is.
Mom: A connoisseur is someone who knows all about something and loves it.
Reese: I don't know about Skittles, but I'm a **mommy** connoisseur.

Terra

Remember how, when children are very young, they believe moms know everything? Our oldest son was six when he came home from school and recited the Pledge of Allegiance. "I pledge allegiance to the flag of the United States of America and to the republic of Richard Stans." I pointed out that it should be "for which it stands," and he insisted that the teacher knew more than me and that Richard Stans is correct. That was the beginning of the end of "Mommy knows everything."

Cathy

Children sometimes use the wrong words, especially if they have similar syllables. My son confused the words "cemetery" and "cafeteria." Hence, a few of our elderly friends were buried in cafeterias, while we often dined at the cemetery. He also combined words and coined a few of his own: "eyebrashes" was his word for eyebrows, and "ash-lies" was his word for eyelashes.

Trish

As a toddler, Sydney's bedtime prayers consisted of "Ad doo wada wada wok, eeda umda uda prumpy do." She said that exact phrasing every night for years, and though we never knew what it meant, we were sure God did.

Mommy's Little Helps
ORGANIZATIONAL TIPS

KAREN
Keep a wall calendar. Make everyone responsible
for recording his or her scheduled activities on it.

TRISH
Place wooden crates under your end tables or coffee table
to store miscellaneous toys, books, or clutter. You can clean
up in a snap, and kids have what they need in a pinch.

LESLIE
Color code your kiddos: toothbrush, comb or hairbrush, towels, laundry
baskets, ink color on a calendar, stickers on steps, and sticky notes to them.
You could even embroider a few X's in the toes of socks or mark with a Sharpie.
They'll be able to tell what belongs to them much more easily. Added bonus:
You know who's forgetting to put away their stuff. And so will they!

TERRA
When you're running late because a child is moving slowly, make getting out the door
a game by saying, "I bet I can put on my shirt before you put on your shirt." Most kids
will run to put on their shirt. "I bet I can get ready to go and stand at the front door
before you do" can motivate a child to speedy action so you will leave on time.

CATHY
If you think your home will have perfect order, engrave these words on the front
door, and then you'll never have to make excuses for messes: "Fasten your seatbelts.
We're experiencing a little turbulence" (quote from Stephanie Pierson).

Life's Amens

By Cathy Messecar

Jolie, our barely three-year-old granddaughter, asked me to read to her, and she chose a book about a whimsical farm tractor. While I read, she held the book and turned the shiny cardboard pages. The tractor carried on quite a monologue about his "nine to five" fieldwork. She skipped some of the pages, not showing interest in mechanical issues. After six pages, the tractor said, "And my dependable motor. . . ."

We didn't get any further. Jolie closed the book and said, "Amen!" Later that day, she brought me the Little Golden Book *Sleeping Beauty*. As I read to her, she tolerated the storyline a bit better—maybe because it involved a princess, an evil rival, and a handsome prince. Again, when we closed the book, she said, "Amen!"

I recall that the "Amen" at the end of prayers was one of the first words my children mimicked. Later, as their vocabularies grew, so did the lists of things they were thankful for—Dad, Mom, cats, dogs, and all the little fishes in the deep blue sea. At mealtimes, my children expressed fresh faith when they gave thanks for rice, water, ketchup, salt, pepper, and the dinner plates.

As children trained in prayer grow up, the world encroaches, and their knowledge of good and evil develops. As concerns deepen, we witnessed them pray for victims of tragedies. Adults have told me that they've come full circle in their prayer lives because of hearing children's prayers. Our eyes, open to the rips and tears in the world's character, get back in tune with God who also cares about salt, pepper, rice, and dinner plates.

My granddaughter Jolie finally learned to say "The end" when closing a book instead of "Amen." But, I remember—and rather like—that we shared an activity that ended with an "Amen." A little blessing tacked onto family activities is always a good thing.

Yummy, Yummy in My Tummy
BREAKFASTS

TERRA
SMOOTHIE

Fruit smoothies are popular at our house, and the ingredients are simple. Put in the blender a cup of plain yogurt or milk, a half cup of fruit juice, a small banana, and a cup of other fruit—fresh or frozen—like blueberries, strawberries, raspberries, or mango. Blend for a minute or two, and breakfast is ready.

IRISH
BAKED FRENCH TOAST
(A make-ahead breakfast for busy mornings)

⅔ cup packed brown sugar	½ cup butter, melted	2 cups milk
2 teaspoons ground cinnamon	6-8 eggs, lightly beaten	1 loaf Texas toast bread

Combine brown sugar and cinnamon. Spread evenly over the bottom of a greased jelly roll pan. Drizzle melted butter over top of the sugar mixture. Combine milk and eggs in mixing bowl. Dip each slice of bread in and soak, then lay on top of sugar mixture in single layer over entire pan. Pour any remaining egg mixture over top of slices. Bake uncovered at 350 degrees for 25-30 minutes until golden brown.

CATHY

EGGS AND BACON IN A MUFFIN TIN

12 slices of thick bacon   12 eggs

Lightly spray with cooking spray the cups of a nonstick muffin pan. Line each cup with a slice of bacon. Crack eggs one at a time and pour contents into a muffin cup. Prick the yolks, and salt and pepper the eggs. Cook for 40–50 minutes at 350 degrees until yolk is done. Serves 8 to 12 people.

LESLIE

BREAKFAST TACOS

In Texas, breakfast tacos rule! Load bacon, scrambled eggs, and cheese onto a warm flour tortilla. Variations include chorizo, queso, sausage, and sautéed potato and onion. Serve as-is or with salsa or jalapeño ranch dressing. Added bonus: They keep warm for a long time when wrapped in foil.

KAREN

NEW, IMPROVED BREAKFAST CEREAL

Favorite breakfast cereals are usually high in sugar. To cut down on sugar intake and still keep some of the colorful, fun "kibbles and bits," mix a little healthy whole grain cereal in the box. When the kids pour it out, they'll think it's a new variety.

Mama Sez

*Before I got married I had six theories about bringing up children
and now I have six children and no theories.*

—JOHN WILMOT

Children Just Can't Keep Still

BY LESLIE WILSON

When North Texas experienced a break from the typical scorching July temperatures, my husband, Bret, suggested our family watch a movie outside on the trampoline to enjoy the crisp night air.

Though it sounded good, this was no simple undertaking. It took us nearly an hour to gather the requisite materials: laptop computer for viewing, DVD, extension cord, bedding, snacks, flashlights, bug spray.

Finally, Bret and I, along with our first grader and two preschoolers, congregated on our round trampoline and snuggled close. Not intentionally—the weight of bodies and equipment made everything sink into the middle of the trampoline. After many attempts to get comfortable, Bret begged, "Why can't you kids just be still?"

Was he kidding? Had he not been around our children before? He seemed to have forgotten that children are born with a wiggle gene.

They're destined to move incessantly from birth until they become teenagers and we need them to mow the lawn and drive younger siblings to basketball practice. *Then*, whether sleeping, watching TV, or chatting on the computer, all they'll want to do is be still.

Word Quilters' Wisdom

HELPING OUT WITH CHORES

KAREN

Kids can easily put away their toys, art supplies, books, and other belongings in a closet or under their beds using dollar store plastic bins (with lids) that stack neatly.

TRISH

Hold a chore auction. As children complete the required chores on time with a positive attitude, they earn tickets. Once a week (or month), hold an auction and let them use their tickets to bid on items like toys, an extra hour of TV, a later bedtime, or an ice cream cone.

LESLIE

Chore charts worked great for us. As my kids got older, they visualized the charts in their heads, thinking of what they needed to do next.

CATHY

In an experiment televised on PBS, several modern families returned to pioneer times and lived for months without electricity or current methods of food preserving. The family members took pride in their work that helped sustain the family. They saw the benefit of working as a team. Personal satisfaction and character develop when children successfully complete chores and receive kudos for their contribution to the family.

TERRA

Doing chores benefits children as it helps them gain self-confidence and makes it clear that they are contributing to the family. At two, our sons could put their toys away. By three, they could feed the cat. By four and five, they made their own beds and cleared the table.

CHAPTER SEVEN

Ordinary Moments

Mama Sez

The one thing children wear out faster than shoes is parents.

—JOHN J. PLOMP

You Might Be a Mommy If . . .

- You've paid your son to eat "yucky" broccoli at Grandma's house.
- You regularly shower with naked Barbies.
- Your stomach hangs out over your jeans, and you've never had a beer.
- You start every other sentence with "Because . . ."
- You buy groceries on Monday and finish putting them away on Tuesday.
- Your children are better dressed than you.
- You've ever exclaimed, "How on earth did *that* get in there?" when your preschooler finds his artwork in the trash.
- You drive a minivan with a "Baby on Board" decal—and your youngest is six.

Word Quilters' Wisdom

TEACHING CHILDREN TO BE RESPONSIBLE

KAREN

When our boys were old enough to trust alone for a short time, we began by leaving them at home for ten minutes at a time. Often we just drove around the block.

LESLIE

A mature person takes responsibility for his or her actions and behaviors—and doesn't pass the buck or blame someone else. If your child loses a friend's toy, he or she should offer to replace it. You can help by offering your child extra chores to do to pay off the debt. Kids need age-appropriate mishaps and disappointments to help prepare them for bigger ones later in life. If we always shield, always protect, always swoop in and save the day, they never learn how to stand on their own.

CATHY

In elementary school, my son, Russell, kept forgetting his lunch money. He didn't suffer any consequences because I would take the money to the school. One day when he forgot, tough love prevailed. He phoned begging me to bring him the coins, but I said, "Russell, you figure out what to do." He asked the cafeteria lady for a free lunch, but he had to take double the money the next day. You guessed it. He never forgot his lunch money after that.

TERRA

It helps kids learn responsibility when you strike a happy medium between giving orders and being a helicopter parent. Finding that middle ground in your parenting style allows kids to learn, make mistakes, and grow. You can help your toddler learn responsibility by having her put her book away after story time, or sing silly songs together as you give the dog a bath or feed the goldfish with her help.

TRISH

Let your children help you, and allow them to make mistakes. I am a perfectionist, and it is difficult to let go. But I have learned to allow my children to do their own chores, like putting their clothes away, even though they don't fold everything in perfect squares.

The First Day of School

By Leslie Wilson

*A*fter I peeled my young son from my left thigh and left him in his new classroom, I walked into the elementary school library to attend my first Boo Hoo Breakfast. The special event is designed to give kindergarten moms an outlet for their grief and allow them to connect with other moms in a similar situation.

I walked over to one young mom who looked miserable.

"Are you going to be okay?" I asked.

"I guess. I just don't know what I should do."

How true! After years of diapering, wiping, feeding, cleaning, burping, bathing, changing, playing, reading, and putting him down for a nap, a mom's arms can feel mighty empty when her child goes to kindergarten. It doesn't really matter if it's the first, middle, last, twins, or an only—you struggle with what exactly you should do with your time.

Some of you may not be ready.

Some of you might have been praying about and preparing for your freedom since nine months before that baby was born.

Whatever your stance, you're undergoing a major change.

Life may never be the same as you get your first taste of the empty nest. Truth is, it doesn't always taste good.

But from a mom who's been there, here's some free advice for the faint of heart who may be tempted to spend all of their waking hours "helping" the kindergarten teacher create die cut pumpkins.

Limit your volunteer hours. You'll be surprised how quickly your schedule will fill up. Find one or two areas where you'd like to work—not just the ones where teachers or moms are begging for help—and stick with those.

Pursue some hobbies. Remember those things you used to do before you had kids? Thought not. Figure out what those things are and dive in. They'll revive and challenge your mind once again.

Work out. Make time for this every morning . . . or afternoon. It'll make your heart—and head—feel better.

Take your husband or a friend to lunch. You'll feel like a big girl again.

Redo something around the house. Paint is cheap. You've wanted to make some changes, and now you have the time.

Now that you have some free time, don't just languish. But don't spend every waking hour at the school, either. Find a balance between being a mom and being a person.

Turn your Boo Hoo into Woo Hoo!

DEALING WITH ILLNESS OR INJURY

KAREN

Remember to line small wastebaskets with plastic bags when stomach flu hits the family. If a child gets sick during the night, it makes cleanup go much quicker.

TERRA

When my three-year-old son fell and cut his knee, I cleaned and bandaged it. I repeatedly told him how sorry I was—meaning I wished he hadn't gotten hurt. As moms, we endeavor to protect our little ones from every boo-boo or illness, no matter how slight. My son told me, "Mom, why are you sorry? It's not your fault." Sometimes our kids are smarter than we are.

LESLIE

Many times, our children take their cues from our behavior. If I cry hysterically when my daughter gets a gash on her forehead, that's going to scare her worse than if I reassure her with soothing tones. It's worth the extra effort to remain composed.

CATHY

Invest in a book for childhood medical emergencies. To find quick answers to your questions from bee stings to broken bones, here's a favorite: *A Parent's Guide to Medical Emergencies: First Aid for Your Child* by Janet Zand, Rachel Walton, and Robert Rountree.

TRISH

When your children get sick, collect a few of their favorite DVDs and spread sleeping bags on the floor—for both of you. Forget your schedule, and just focus on being a mom. That's what they need most.

Mama Sez

My mother had a great deal of trouble
with me, but I think she enjoyed it.

—MARK TWAIN

Nourishment for Mom's Spirit

Listen, my [child], to your father's instruction
and do not forsake your mother's teaching.

PROVERBS 1:8

KAREN

CHEESE FACE SANDWICH

Top a piece of toast with a slice of cheese. Use sliced, pimento-stuffed olives for eyes, green or yellow sliced pepper for eyebrows, a slice of carrot for a nose, and sliced red pepper for a mouth. For hair, use curly pieces of celery or carrots shredded with a potato peeler.

TERRY

CHOCOLATE CHIP MARSHMALLOW BANANAS

This is a fun recipe for children age two and up to make when camping or for the grill in your backyard. All you need are bananas, chocolate chips, miniature marshmallows, and aluminum foil. Slice an unpeeled banana lengthwise, but not all the way through, creating a pocket for the chocolate chips. Fill the pocket with one-fourth cup of chocolate chips and some marshmallows and wrap in aluminum foil. Mom or Dad can put them on the grill or a campfire for four minutes, then turn and cook another four minutes. Let them cool, and then eat this dessert with a spoon.

CATHY

SPRINKLE COOKIES

Granddaughter Jolie, age four, loved to bake cookies when she visited me. During one visit, I had limited time when she asked to bake cookies. So I sat her down at the kitchen table with plenty of room and gave her a box of vanilla wafers, a bowl of bought frosting, and a variety of sprinkles. Content, she frosted and decorated for nearly an hour. When I took her home, friends were visiting her tween brothers. The four boys pounced on her plate of frosted cookies. A young guest was overheard saying, "Your sister sure is a good cook." In a pinch, this is a tasty treat for little ones and a fun activity.

KID OMELETS

My son enjoys breakfast more than any other meal, so I taught him to make scrambled eggs at a fairly young age. As long as he told me he would be using the stove, I allowed him the freedom to cook eggs unsupervised after he mastered the process. One morning, I heard him talking to a friend who had spent the night. "Austin, would you like me to make you an omelet?" Suddenly, scrambled eggs had become omelets!

To make, brown sausage or crumble a few slices of bacon in a nonstick pan. Add three eggs, well-beaten with a little milk, salt, and pepper. Sprinkle cheese over the top, and cook over medium-low heat until the runny egg firms up. Fold over to make a half-moon. Serve with toast and orange juice.

HOMEMADE STRAWBERRY ICE CREAM

1 (10 ounce) package
  frozen strawberries

½ cup white sugar
⅔ cup heavy cream

Combine the frozen strawberries and sugar in a food processor or blender and blend until smooth. Add cream until blended well. Serve immediately, or freeze for up to one week.

Mommy's Little Helps
DISCIPLINE TIPS

LESLIE
When giving preschoolers a directive, make sure you have their attention. Don't just shout out to thin air, "Get your cleats; it's time to leave for soccer." Instead, squat down in front of your child, so you can look directly in his eyes. Cup his chin. Say his name first, then give the "assignment." Finally, add on the consequence in case he doesn't obey. Example: "Reese, our friends will be here in two minutes. Please put away your train. If you don't obey, I'll take away the train set, and you won't be allowed to play with it for a whole week. Do you understand me?" Then—and this is the biggest part—follow through!

KAREN
When we were in a store, the kids had to keep their hands
in their pockets. If hands came out, we left the store.

TRISH
If your child misbehaves while you're at someone else's house, quietly ask your child to join you in a separate room. Discuss the issue, outline the consequences, and stay with your child during the time out. This technique won't embarrass your child or your host.

CATHY
Make sure that children help pay for repairs when they carelessly damage something in the household or a neighbor's property. Let them help compare prices, make new purchases, and assist in mending "fences." This teaches them that their actions—intentional or not—have consequences.

TERRA
Children listen and learn when we're consistent with routine directives. For example, my husband and I said, "This car isn't starting until all seat belts are buckled." Our children got in this routine and would even remind me to put on my seat belt.

MOM MISCELLANY
ORDINARY MOMENTS

BY TRISH BERG

*L*ife seems full of ordinary moments. Though I wake with high hopes, the reality is that my days are filled with the tedious, not the tantalizing.

Laundry spills out of hampers. Clean clothes pile up on the couch begging to be folded. Bills call out, "Pay me!" And the crud built up on the stovetop has crusted into cement.

Lunches don't pack themselves, nor do dishes wash one another. And what's that unknown food substance crunching on the kitchen floor under my feet?

Errands beckon—get gas, buy groceries, drop off prescriptions, and pick up mail.

I could drown in my ordinary moments. Or, at the very least, allow them to render me stressed out, bitter, and frustrated.

Because I forget that the ordinary moments define me as a mom. They show how much I love my husband and my children—people God has placed in my life because he trusts me to care for them.

When I take time to recognize the extraordinary people around me, the tedious becomes tantalizing.

CHAPTER EIGHT

Milestones

Mama Sez

Most of all the other beautiful things in life come by twos and threes,
by dozens and hundreds. Plenty of roses, stars, sunsets, rainbows,
brothers and sisters, aunts and cousins, comrades and friends—
but only one mother in the whole world.

—Kate Douglas Wiggin

A Few of Our Favorite Things
GIFT FROM MY CHILD

Terra

I treasure handmade gifts! I still have a card on my desk that one of my sons
made for me in kindergarten. It reads: "Mom of the world." Though the card's
colors have faded through the years, I trust the sentiment remains true.

CATHY

My daughter's second grade teacher furnished each child with a greenware (unbaked ceramic) two-inch-tall baby bird, with mouth opened wide. Each child painted the beak yellow and put two black dots for eyes. The teacher then fired the birds in a kiln. Sheryle proudly presented the tiny, begging bird to me, saying, "Its mouth holds toothpicks." It reminds me of her dedicated love back then and now, as she mothers her own little ones.

KAREN

My son nailed some boards together to make a shelf in the cupboard where I stored my pots and pans so I wouldn't have to stack them up so high. It wasn't fancy, but it organized my cupboard perfectly.

TRISH

My family gifts me with a guilt-free afternoon nap on Mother's Day. After church and lunch, I get to crawl in bed and sleep as long as I want. It's the best gift ever!

LESLIE

Every Mother's Day and Christmas, I receive the same special gift from my youngest son. Reese looks up the guitar chords on the Internet and teaches himself to play a song he knows I'll like. These private concerts mean far more than anything he could buy for me.

SIMPLE RECIPE THAT KIDS LOVE

BAKED POTATO HAYSTACKS | BY TRISH BERG

10 potatoes
1 head lettuce
1 large onion
1 (16 ounce) bag of baby
 carrots

1 (13 ounce) bag Doritos,
 crushed
2 pounds lean ground
 beef, browned and
 drained
1 (18 ounce) can sloppy joe
 sauce

1 (28 ounce) can pork and
 beans
2 (10¾ ounce) cans cream
 of mushroom soup
2 tablespoons milk
1 pound Velveeta cheese

Bake potatoes in the oven at 400 degrees for about an hour until tender. Shred lettuce; chop onion and carrots fine. Put each vegetable in a separate serving bowl with a spoon. Set aside. Place crushed Doritos in a separate serving bowl with a spoon. Set aside. In a saucepan, combine ground beef, sloppy joe sauce, and pork and beans; heat until bubbly. Keep warm. In a separate saucepan, dilute cream of mushroom soup with milk and Velveeta cheese on low heat until well blended. Keep warm. At serving time, have guests begin with their baked potato on a large plate, sliced open and mashed with a fork. As they walk down the buffet line, they top their potato with the toppings of their choice in this order: sloppy joe, lettuce, onions, carrots, and cheese sauce, ending with Doritos. Serves 10 people.

The First Time They Sing the Boredom Blues

By Terra Hangen

"Mom, there's nothing to do." Oh, the dreaded whine that no mom wants to hear.

When "nothing to do" threatened, our sons perfected the art of indoor camping, creating a tent with blankets and sheets covering the dining table. They each invited a friend or two, scrounged up pillows and blankets and flashlights, and the afternoon and evening entertainment began.

My parents created a house where my friends and I liked to hang out, and my husband and I fashioned the same kind of home for our kids and their friends. Since we didn't buy fancy furnishings, we didn't mind getting a few dings or stains on furniture, rugs, or walls.

We preferred having five or six or more noisy and rambunctious boys playing at our house, where we could keep loose tabs on them, rather than having them play less supervised elsewhere.

Much to our shock and dismay, after a sleepover at a friend's house, one of our young sons announced that they watched the Playboy TV channel. That provided a real incentive to encourage kids to spend time at our house.

A main ingredient for successful kid gatherings at our house was having plenty of food and drink available. Bread, peanut butter, bananas, fruit juice, and sodas turned our typically quiet home into a noisy Mecca for energized kids. They needed a lot of fuel for all that running, jumping, and bike riding. In summer, cold watermelon and homemade popsicles attract children like magnets. And did I mention tortilla chips and salsa? Our air pop popcorn maker made lots of inexpensive and healthy popcorn very quickly.

We kept sports equipment around, including a badminton set, baseball bats and extra mitts, soccer balls, and some tennis racquets and balls for the court at the park across the street. The equipment got banged up pretty quickly and even got lost, so we found good sources for used sports equipment.

In good weather, the sports equipment drew kids like honey attracts bees, and indoor camping was popular all year 'round. I encourage you to try these ideas—and maybe you won't hear, "Mom, there's nothing to do."

Mama Sez

If you would have your son to walk honorably through the world, you must not attempt to clear the stones from his path, but teach him to walk firmly over them—not insist upon leading him by the hand, but let him learn to go alone.

—ANNE BRONTË

A Few of Our Favorite Things
OUTDOOR ACTIVITY

KAREN
Swimming at our community lake provided great summer afternoon fun
for my kids and a chance for me to have fellowship with other moms.

TERRA
When your family visits the beach or walks along a stream or in the woods,
gather smooth rocks and wipe them clean in preparation for rock painting. All you
need is acrylic paint in tubes, some cheap paint brushes, and the rocks. Very young
children should use tempera paint. Paint the rocks outside on the grass or at a table,
and wear a smock since acrylic paint stains clothes. Have your kids paint anything
from the name of their favorite sports team to ladybugs, frogs, and flowers.

TRISH
Living in north central Ohio where autumn is filled with orange
and red leaves and cool breezes, we love biking as a family on our
local bike trails. It's a free family activity, it's great exercise, and you can
easily pack a picnic lunch and enjoy a sweet autumn day in the park.

LESLIE
Growing up in Evergreen, Colorado, I always dreamed that my family would
learn how to ski and enjoy it as much as I did. When I settled outside the Dallas
area, my hopes faded a tad. But we managed to visit relatives back home often
enough to help make that dream come true. There's just nothing like skiing all
day, warming by the fire afterward, downing chili, hot-tubbing, and swapping
wipeout stories. Plus, now my kids can ski circles around me, which I love!

CATHY

Outdoor picnics rank at the top of the list for our children. We have a lovely, deep-banked creek with shallow water that winds its way through one hundred acres. Our children loved to picnic on the small, shaded sandbars at the bottom of the gully. "Picturesque" doesn't do justice to the cool, fifteen-feet-deep gully with exposed gnarled roots of the overhanging trees. It looked like gnomes, fairies, and trolls could all find homes among those intertwined and knobby roots. My children, and often their guests, enjoyed hours of fun searching for arrowheads and anything identifiable that had washed downstream since the last storm.

Where in the World Is Geo Georgie?

By Trish Berg

Since I'm the mother of four children ages sixteen to nine, I have become sort of a homework expert. I have been through third grade four times, sixth grade three times, eighth grade two times, and tenth grade once. And that doesn't even include my own education through high school and college.

I know my ABCs, 1-2-3s, and even a few select words in French and Spanish. I know my Big Foot Word Challenge words. I study spelling words with my elementary students each and every week. And I've taken geometry four times.

But lest you think that's all, I've made a single-serve chocolate milk carton into an armadillo four times, once for each child in the first grade. Each time, I think, "Oh, I'll just keep this one for the next child who needs it." But I am an honest mom, so I don't.

I have mailed off and tracked Geo Georgie, a paper character who travels the world. And during each child's fifth grade year, when the Living Biography project comes around, I put together costumes for John Stith Pemberton (the inventor of Coca-Cola), Anastasia Romanov (the Russian princess), and Nellie Bly (one of the first female journalists).

Kids and homework. Homework and kids. They don't always go together like cookies and milk. (Though serving cookies and milk while doing homework some-times helps.)

There is no easy way around homework. It can drag you down if you let it. It can steal your evenings and your family's sanity.

I don't always get it right, but I have learned to provide dedicated family time to work on homework at the kitchen table. We sit together while my children work on their assignments. I make it fun by serving a snack they love and allowing them breaks as needed to go out and shoot some hoops, play on the Wii, or watch an episode of *iCarly*.

Yes, I have become sort of a homework expert. Not that I want to be a homework expert, but with four children, I've had no choice. All in all, I have, hmmm, let's see, forty-nine years of education including theirs and mine. That's a lot of schooling!

Yet I am still not sure where in the world Geo Georgie is.

Nourishment for Mom's Spirit

As Jesus was saying these things, a woman in the crowd called out,
"Blessed is the mother who gave you birth and nursed you."

LUKE 11:27

Mommy's Little Helps

TRAVEL TIPS

TERRA

When your family is driving on a road trip, have your kids count
something that they see. In farm country this can be barns, horses,
or cows, and on city streets or highways they can count cars of a color they
choose. The first to see ten cows or ten blue cars, or their chosen target, wins.
No prize is needed; just let them choose what to count and begin a new game.

TRISH

Play musical chairs. If your kids argue about who sits where on a road trip, number each
seat and place those in a jar. At each stop (for a meal or a potty break at a rest stop),
have everyone draw a number and sit in that seat. Change seats as often as you need to.

Cathy

DVD players give parents—especially the driver—a break from chatter or chaos, but they can't take the place of family fun. When children are adults, they will more likely remember the interaction and stunts pulled by family members than movies they watched on a trip. Pack individually marked crayon boxes, books, and tablet puzzles for each child into a gallon-size plastic zipper bag with the child's name on it.

Karen

Prepare a bag full of fun puzzles, coloring pages, or short stories. Many can be downloaded and printed from kids' show websites. Take along a lap desk.

Leslie

On long trips, we did thirty-minute rotations. Our kids could listen to music, read, color, play Game Boy, play with window clings, or do another favorite activity. After thirty minutes, they had to stop that activity and choose a different one. That always left them wanting more instead of complaining that they were bored.

A Piercing Scream

By Leslie Wilson

*M*y daughter got her ears pierced for her ninth birthday. To honor that milestone, everyone on the planet bought her a multi-pack of inexpensive earrings from Wal-Mart. The thinking: if she loses one, it won't matter since each pair was so cheap to begin with. That's the good news. The bad news is that Molly, who struggles to keep up with two socks for a whole day, had more than thirty pairs of earrings to store, wear, and keep track of.

That's an awfully tall order for a . . . shall we say . . . organizationally challenged tween.

To prepare for stepping on future misplaced jewelry, I walked around barefoot for months, hoping to toughen the soles of my feet to withstand stepping on studs or backs without piercing through tender skin on the balls of my feet.

I knew Molly would lose them. That was as certain as death, taxes, and shocking behavior on the MTV awards.

Why the certainty? Besides the fact that my favorite daughter (okay, you got me, she's my only daughter) is prone to losing things—her tiny clutch purses, money, homework assignments, the aforementioned socks, sheet music, library books . . . well, you get the idea—those darned earrings were so tiny that anyone might be prone to lose one or two on occasion.

Also, Molly has carpet in her bedroom and bathroom sink area.

You do the math.

So, rather than getting angry if I were to tread on a trinket, I embraced this new phase—fully expecting I *would* have Swiss cheese feet. That way, if I didn't, I'd be pleasantly surprised.

In Molly's case, the apple didn't fall very fall from the tree. She comes from a long line of women who excel in a unique method of disorganization. We know right where everything is—most of the time—but we drive those around us crazy with our trademark chaos.

I figure my mom must have wished I'd grow up and have a daughter just like me, which I did. As a mother, I find myself telling Molly she must clean up her room before she has the freedom to watch TV or go to a friend's house. In these days of calm before the teenage storm, her inherited brand of organized chaos remains our only real battle.

And then we added 262 pea-sized earrings.

Word Quilters' Wisdom

TEACHING KIDS ABOUT FINANCES

TERRA

When your child has some money saved, find a local bank that encourages children to have accounts with no (or a low) minimum deposit and no fees. Children as young as five find interest in saving money if you take them to open an account in person.

KAREN

Set up jars labeled **tithe**, **savings**, **spending**. Determine how much of the allowance should go into each jar. The tithe goes to church. They may use the money in the spending jar for things they want to buy. They can use the savings jar to save for something special.

TRISH

Live it first. Your children are watching how you handle money, and they are learning from you. A fantastic resource for families is the *ABC's of Handling Money God's Way* by Crown Financial Ministries (available at www.crown.org).

LESLIE

Match whatever they can save in their very own 401(k) for kids. This teaches children the power of denying immediate gratification, saving to buy what you want, and never using credit.

CATHY

A tween grandson saw me preparing to make a bank deposit and tallying cash. He asked, "How much money does Pop make?" I told him what our family business brings in, and asked in return, "What does Pop spend money on to stay in business?" My response gave him an early lesson in assets and liabilities. The discussion led to the expenses of running a household. These frank discussions aid elementary age children to better understand why parents sometimes say no to their purchase requests.

CHAPTER NINE

Gifts

Mama Sez

A man loves his sweetheart the most, his wife the best, but his mother the longest.

—IRISH PROVERB

FAMILY SNAPSHOT

"Quiet!" Screamed the Teacher

BY KAREN ROBBINS

When my third son entered second grade, they tested his reading skills. He fell into a borderline area where the evaluators thought it best to require him to enter a tutoring program supported by federal funds. Because of my connection to the PTA, I knew that the program needed him more than he needed it. Federally funded programs lose their grants if there are not enough participants to justify them. But I welcomed the opportunity for him to escape his classroom twice a week for the reading program. Why? His classroom teacher was a screamer.

One of my regular volunteer projects in the school put me in a room just down the hall from my son's second grade classroom. Whenever the teacher felt a bit overwhelmed, she resorted to her fallback method of discipline—screaming and yelling at her students. I could hear her.

On the other hand, the reading program had a teacher who was innovative, reassuring, and, above all, patient. She instilled in my son a love for learning and certainly reinforced his reading skills.

That year proved difficult for a second grader who wasn't used to the kind of discipline his classroom teacher handed out. However, it gave us an opportunity to talk often about how people did things in different ways. We worked at being kind to the teacher because perhaps she needed kindness more than anything else. Down the road, when he encountered other teachers whose personalities didn't quite fit his, we worked through it in much the same way. I hoped he would learn to cope with those in authority who might be difficult. I wanted him to exercise good people skills so later in life he would remember to treat people with respect and courtesy.

Today, as an adult, he manages a group of people who seem to appreciate his leadership. Perhaps that second grade teacher and his tutor taught him more than just reading, writing, and arithmetic.

You Might Be a Mommy If . . .

- You can make the coolest Halloween costume ever out of aluminum foil, an old tablecloth, duct tape, and a toilet paper tube.
- Your four-year-old daughter enters the room, hands behind her back, saying, "Open your mouth and close your eyes."
- You've asked your pediatrician how much gum your child would have to swallow to plug up his intestines.
- You've helped your kids make a baking soda and vinegar volcano, a salt map, and an "All About Me" poster—this school year alone!
- You consider PB&J and Cheetos a nutritious meal.
- You unclog your toilet at least once a day.
- You can change from lounging-around-the-house-in-sweats casual to dressed-up-for-a-night-on-the-town glamorous in three and a half minutes.
- You have four children in your minivan and consider it a light load.

Home Run Hitter

By Trish Berg

When my nine-year-old son, Colin, hit his first home run, not only was I one proud mama, but you should have seen the look on his face as he watched the baseball sail past the right fielder and into next week.

His entire team and all of his coaches greeted him at home plate with high-fives.

What an evening for the Berg clan! One I will never forget. The team gave Colin the home run ball, and we have since written on it with a permanent marker: "June 16, 2009—Colin Berg's First Homerun." I think Colin slept with that baseball for a few nights. Now it sits on our shelf for all to see.

Up until that night, it had been a very long baseball season for Colin. He struck out most of the time from not swinging. And he didn't swing because he feared striking out. Caught in a vicious cycle, I think he stepped into the batter's box each time praying for a walk.

This season, his first year in player pitch, added the fear of getting hit with a ball thrown directly at him at fifty miles per hour.

Now Colin is a home run hitter, something that can never be taken away from him. Despite striking out all season long, being afraid of the ball, and feeling frustrated and upset, he never gave up. Every Sunday evening, he worked on his hitting with his dad at the ball field. We constantly reminded him that we were proud of him for doing his best no matter what his batting average.

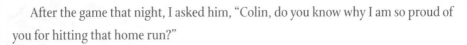

After the game that night, I asked him, "Colin, do you know why I am so proud of you for hitting that home run?"

"Because I never gave up."

I know my son will strike out again. And he may or may not send another hit out of the ball park. But home run hitters never give up, no matter what curve ball life throws at them.

Mama Sez

Insanity is hereditary; you get it from your children.

—SAM LEVENSON

Word Quilters' Wisdom

TREATING KIDS AS UNIQUE INDIVIDUALS

TERRA
Our two sons have always enjoyed different interests and skills. One enjoys the outdoors, trucks, and motorcycles. The other son is lead vocalist in a band and rides a bicycle. Both of them enjoy camping and hiking. We notice what each son likes and celebrate that, which makes family gatherings lots of fun.

LESLIE
Comparing the personality types to characters from Charles Schultz's *Peanuts* helps me remember the unique qualities of each: Choleric Lucy; Melancholy Charlie Brown; Phlegmatic Linus; Sanguine Sally. By celebrating the positive aspects of each and minimizing the not-so-great qualities, we nurture our kids' growth and help them discover their potential. For example, everyone thinks of Lucy as bossy, but she can certainly organize a group and get things done.

CATHY
Even if you live in a crowded home, try to give each child his or her own space, even if it's just a five-dollar cubicle to store personal stuff and to decorate to his or her liking.

KAREN
Nothing showed me more about how different children are than raising twins. God has made each one unique. Applaud the gifts he's given each child, and don't imply one gift is better than the other.

TRISH
Schedule individual dates with your children. Mike and I rotate seasons. He takes each of our children on individual dates in the summer and winter, and I do the same in the fall and spring. Let them pick what you do on the date, and enjoy getting to know each of your children one on one.

Her children arise and call her blessed.

PROVERBS 31:28

MOM MISCELLANY
WHEN I'M NINETY

BY TRISH BERG

When I'm ninety, I hope I smile a lot. I hope I look at the sunshine, hear the birds sing, and thank the Lord for another day this side of heaven. I hope I appreciate the gifts I've been given, the people who've loved me, and the life I've lived. And when each storm of life passes my way, when the thunder rolls and the lightning strikes, I hope I ride it out by remembering all the good times I've enjoyed.

When I'm ninety, I hope my kids still come around to see me. Maybe they'll bring me cookies and milk, like I used to do for them after school. I hope they forgive me for all my motherly mistakes, and remember all the good stuff from their childhood.

Dial Tone

By Leslie Wilson

"Can I get a cell phone?" Molly asked for the fortieth time last month.

"Sure," I answered. "How are you going to pay for it?"

Flustered, she stammered, "I mean, can *you* get me a cell phone?"

"If you mean 'will I buy you a cell phone and add you to our monthly plan which already costs Dad and me $100 a month,' the answer is no."

"But—" she started, and then stopped, as my head whipped toward her, my best are-you-really-going-to-press-the-issue look boring into her.

Not easily daunted, she tried another tack.

"Mom, how old were you when you got a cell phone?"

This is an easy one. Actually, I'm glad she asked. "Thirty-seven," I trumped.

"Oh." End of conversation.

The cell phone battle has become the argument du jour. About once a month, one of my children insists their lives won't be complete until they're wireless.

I insist back that they'll be fine.

"But everybody else has one," Charlie laments.

"Are you kidding me?" I stare at him, mouth gaping that he would dare try that lame line in an effort to persuade me.

Truth be told, a huge percentage of students at his middle school do carry cell phones. Though they're not allowed to use them during school hours, I see kids chatting away during pickup—probably talking to their friends fifteen feet away.

Charlie often borrows a friend's phone to call us when coaches have let them out of practice early. I tell him to be thankful that God gave him such good friends who loan him their phones.

Who's paying for these things is what I want to know. I see many kids with camera phones accessorized to the hilt—with cool covers and earpieces I'd like to have. They're playing games or taking pictures of friends. The phone has become a form of entertainment in and of itself.

If all else fails, and I feel cellular weakness coming on, I can always remind Molly of the time I passed on my old phone to her. She was gathering spy stuff—surveillance equipment—to satisfy her inquiring (read: nosy) nature. Armed with headset, hip belt, and phone, she dashed outside to play spy.

Thirty minutes later, she skulked back in, eyes red and puffy, shoulders shaking.

"What on earth is the matter?" I asked, taking her in my arms, trying to calm her down as best I could.

"I accidentally called 9-1-1."

Accidentally? How do you accidentally dial three numbers? Instead of harping on minute details, a nagging thought took hold.

I vaguely remembered someone telling me deactivated cell phones could reach Emergency Services. In fact, churches periodically hold drives to collect old cell phones and chargers to donate to battered women's shelters. My old phone had worked—for that one phone call.

"What happened?" I really wanted—needed—to know.

"The other person said, 'Rockwall County Emergency Services.'"

"What did you do?"

"I hung up."

My husband and I debated whether or not we should call and clarify the situation, to assure EMS we weren't having an emergency. We decided against it since so much time had elapsed.

Everyone in the family, not to mention everyone I saw that day and the next, learned a valuable lesson. Never, ever dial 9-1-1 from any phone unless you have a true emergency.

The silver lining: I was afforded the perfect excuse—Molly's lack of readiness—to not be pressured into getting my children cell phones.

I'm off the hook (no pun intended), for at least a little while longer.

CHAPTER TEN

Lessons

Mama Sez

Children are a great comfort in your old age—and they help you reach it faster, too.

—LIONEL KAUFFMAN

You Might Be a Mommy If . . .

- Your bra size increases, but you can't find one in a 42 long.
- Politics means who is running the PTA.
- Your tween daughter is better dressed than you. Come to think of it, so are her Barbies.
- You've endured leaky tents, burnt hot dogs, and countless mosquito bites because camping is a fun way to make special family memories.
- You feel like a human ATM.
- You've ever informed arguing children, "If you're going to kill each other, do it outside. I just finished cleaning."

The Contest

BY CATHY MESSECAR

*F*amilies usually have a story that's always the first to surface for retelling at family gatherings. Here's ours.

Once upon a blistering hot day in humidity-drenched South Texas, our family worked outside on our one-hundred-acre farm. It always needed tending. Gusty winds caused limbs to fall off trees. Thorn-laden weeds grew up in the corral fencing. Roadside-strewn trash blew into the pastures. Always, always there was something to pick up, mow, or trim on the farm. Our children, Russell and Sheryle, ages eleven and eight, loved being outdoors and helping. They made those days fun by playing in between chores.

One Saturday, our workday had lasted longer than usual. By midafternoon, the children had slacked off their jobs, and a playful mood broke out between the two. They knew that soon the whole family could rush indoors, take showers, and relax in our air-conditioned home. Their jovial moods prompted a few dares from older brother to younger sister: "I bet I can throw a rock farther than you." Naturally, he could, but sister fell for it and entered the contest. Next came the stick toss contest, and after that . . .

Well, that's when the trouble began. Daddy worked about ten feet from the children. He had stripped down to his work boots, jeans, and straw cowboy hat.

Perspiration glistened on his bare back as he bent to his task. Russell turned to his sister with his final test: "I bet I can spit farther than you can."

Sheryle accepted the challenge. She coughed. She sputtered. She mustered all the moisture she could into her mouth and sent the mixture soaring a whopping four feet. Then, Russell tested the wind, harrumphed and collected, leaned forward, his upper body nearly parallel to the ground, and sent a wad soaring in the direction of his dad, never once thinking he could spit that far.

It looked like a pop-up fly ball. The wad of spit kept going and going and going. It seemed I watched in slow motion an impossible miraculous launch. Just at the moment of what should have been landfall, his dad turned around. The winning spittle hit him square on his bare and hairy chest.

"Oh no!" I said.

"Now you're in for it," said Sheryle, pointing her finger at her offending brother.

"Daddy, I didn't mean. . . ." Russell started his apology immediately.

We must have had looks of horror on all three of our faces. The silly predicament, Dad's good nature, and Russell's completed apology caused a wide grin to wreath my husband's face. What could have resulted in a scolding instead turned into a favorite family memory. Relieved, we giggled and teased Dad that now he didn't need a shower after all.

TEACHING KIDS ABOUT SEX

KAREN
Never give more information than is requested by a young child.

TRISH
Keep an ongoing conversation open with your children at every age and stage. Answer their questions when they come up, and share godly books on the subject with them. Two great Focus on the Family books are *Boom: A Guy's Guide to Growing Up* and *Bloom: A Girl's Guide to Growing Up,* both by Michael Ross.

LESLIE
Identify body parts by their real names. Saves everyone confusion later! (Truthfully, we parents are the only ones with hangups or embarrassment in this area.) My oldest son nearly fainted in the bathroom when my husband told him it wasn't really called a pee-pee. Later, he wanted to know if his bottom was really his bottom!

CATHY
We live on a farm with plenty of animals, so procreation questions were normal, as our children witnessed animal births—calves, puppies, kittens. The kids never seemed shy about asking questions; we replied with age-appropriate answers and used proper anatomical names for body parts. Naturally, parents can't foresee all the pitfalls of such frank talk, so our son and daughter both used those proper terms in public before we cautioned them to speak those words only in our household.

TERRA
A good way to ease in conversations about sex is to find age-appropriate books that have your values and read them aloud.

The Game of Life

By Trish Berg

I had a glimpse into the secret of life last Thursday night, and surprisingly enough, my guides were five preteen girls sporting pajamas and fuzzy slippers. We actually played the Game of Life, Milton Bradley-style, and discovered a lot more about each other than we could have realized. My daughters, Hannah and Sydney, had a few friends sleep over, and we spent the night eating popcorn, drinking hot chocolate, and playing board games.

Funny, but life hasn't changed much in the past twenty-five years. Well, the board game, anyway. The board still looks the same, the bridges still don't stay in place, and the little peg people still don't snap into their car seats any better than they did when I was a preteen. You would have thought by now someone would have worked out all the kinks. But like real life, sometimes the kinks are what make life interesting.

So I traveled the path ahead in my little yellow car, feeling young again. The girls all worried about who they would marry and how many children they would have. Because most favored starting their career over going to college, I realized we still need to teach our children virtues like patience and delayed gratification.

When you have a baby in the Life board game, you draw a life card which adds anywhere from fifty thousand dollars to two hundred and fifty thousand dollars to your pot. No one handed me money when I delivered any of my four children. Kids give you many things in life, like squeeze hugs, sloppy kisses, and more love than you could ever imagine. But, the last time I checked, having and raising children drains my bank account—it doesn't increase it.

Another funny thing about the Game of Life? The astronomical amount of money you accumulate. I mean, what's a half million here and there when you have to hire a jockey for your racehorse or attend a Hollywood movie premiere? I chuckled to myself a few nights later as I reconciled our very real checking account and paid our very real bills. I longed for a few of those hundred thousand dollar bills in real life. Too bad they're orange and probably recognizable by any decent bank teller. Guess that means no racehorse or movie premiere for me. I'll just stay home and raise my four little pegs, er, children.

Although I may not have discovered the secret of life, I did learn that life is simpler than we make it out to be, and we find joy in time spent rather than dollars earned. It didn't take a movie premiere to bring joy to five precious girls. All it took was some microwave popcorn, a mug of hot chocolate, and Life.

Nourishment for Mom's Spirit

May your father and mother be glad; may she who gave you birth rejoice!

PROVERBS 23:25

Yummy, Yummy in My Tummy

COOKIE CUTTER COOKIES | BY TERRA HANGEN

Our whole family gets involved in making and decorating cookie cutter cookies for any occasion. Kids as young as two can add sprinkles to the frosting and help with taste testing. We have cookie cutters in every shape imaginable, including flags and stars for the Fourth of July, a turkey for Thanksgiving, hearts for Valentine's Day, and a birthday cake.

Cookies

2 cups sugar	½ cup milk	6 cups flour (start with 5½ cups—then see if it needs more)
1 cup butter	1 teaspoon baking powder	
3 eggs	1 teaspoon vanilla	

Cream sugar and butter until well blended, and then add the sugar and butter to the rest of ingredients. Chill in the refrigerator for two hours.

Roll the chilled dough with a floured rolling pin on a floured sheet of aluminum foil.

Cut out the cookies and bake on a baking sheet lined with a clean sheet of aluminum foil, to prevent burning.

Cook at 350 degrees for 10 to 12 minutes, checking often to see if done. Let the cookies cool completely before frosting them.

Frosting

4 cups confectioner's sugar	½ cup margarine or unsalted butter	5 tablespoons milk

Spread the frosting on cookies and add sprinkles and other decorations right away before the frosting gets hard. Buy lots of sugar sprinkles, chocolate sprinkles, and cinnamon candy and a set of food coloring so you can have bowls of frosting in different colors.

Not a Happy Camper

By Cathy Messecar

I wondered if my ten-year-old son Russell, our homebody child, would last the entire seven-day camp session—his first lengthy time away from home. He left on a Sunday. My first phone call from the camp director came on Monday. The director said my strapping son suffered homesickness. I received similar phone calls on Tuesday and Wednesday. Russell's letter from camp arrived on Thursday.

My usually happy-go-lucky son had addressed the envelope to "Daddy and Momma," scratched it out, and then written, "Mr. and Mrs. Messecar." The scratched-out words ripped through my heart as I released a mother sigh. Opening the letter, I found that Russell, who dwarfed kids his age, had written, "Dear Mommy." Oh my, he never called me mommy.

I soon discovered he had written the sad missive on his first night at camp, instead of playing softball. What? At home, this kid slept with his catcher's mitt. My worry galloped. His letter continued in lament fashion with a few watery stains on the paper. "I wish I hadn't come to camp. I want to see you. I wish I was dead." To his credit, he later made the High School drama team.

By afternoon of the same day the letter arrived, the camp director phoned me again. He said he was an early riser, liked to get up ahead of the kids to have a little quiet time. He said, "I'm *always* the first person awake at camp . . . until this year." It seemed that each morning when the director walked onto his porch, there sat my baby—waiting, loitering, and asking to go home. The director said my friend Dixie, a teacher at camp, was leaving early that afternoon, and Russell could ride home with her if we chose to let him come home a day and a half before closing ceremonies.

My mind wandered back to our earlier preparations for camp: his best friend went with him. Every volunteer knew Russell—bus driver, nurse, cooks. They were his Sunday school teachers, our youth minister, and his friends' parents. The only thing I hadn't done to ensure a successful first summer camp experience was pack his favorite stuffed animal. Though only ten, his height made him look older, and Snoopy poking out of his backpack might have seemed preschoolish.

Most preteens love camp sports, swimming, crafts, badminton, and being with friends, and we knew our son enjoyed those activities. But when his dad and I discussed whether we should make him stick out his camp time or let him come home, my husband said that our son must love his home very much to want to return so badly.

Dad's final words, "If he's that homesick, let him come home."

Little kids aren't that much different from adults. Grownups love the familiar, and we sometimes long to get home even from a relaxing vacation. Children like the coziness and routines of home, too. Any mother knows this to be true because we sing the same songs, reread favorite stories, and play the same games again and again. Until their taste buds mature, children even like to eat the same foods day after day. After many years of mothering, I've learned that at any age or stage of childhood, young or older, repetition is always good—especially when home makes a heart call.

Mama Sez

God could not be everywhere, and, therefore, he made mothers.

—Jewish Proverb

You Might Be a Mommy If . . .

- You're overworked, overcommitted, and underappreciated—and you wouldn't trade your life for anything in the world.
- You understand that children's growth isn't measured by height and weight, or by years, or by a grade in school; it's marked by their progression from "Mommy" to "Mom" to "Mother."
- You blinked, breathed, or turned around, and your kids grew up.

Here's to significant mommy moments—whether firsts or lasts, extraordinary or mundane—to remind us why we do what we do.

We love you, Mom!